THE ECONOMY'S OTHER HALF

The Gendered Economy

Series Editors: Sara Cantillon and Diane Elson

This path-breaking new series critically examines the economy and the theory and methodology of economics through the lens of gender. It will publish original and incisive research that explores the role of gender in the contemporary global economy. The series showcases how economic relationships, actions and institutions are directly affected by gender norms, how a gendered perspective illuminates aspects of the economy that would otherwise be ignored, and challenges many of the tenets that underpin both the mainstream and heterodox interpretation of how economies function.

Published

Collective Bargaining and Gender Equality
Jane Pillinger and Nora Wintour

The Economy's Other Half
James Heintz

The Sex Economy
Monica O'Connor

THE ECONOMY'S OTHER HALF

How Taking Gender Seriously Transforms Macroeconomics

James Heintz

agenda
publishing

First published in 2019 by Agenda Publishing

Agenda Publishing Limited
The Core
Bath Lane
Newcastle Helix
Newcastle upon Tyne
NE4 5TF
www.agendapub.com

ISBN 978-1-78821-063-8

British Library Cataloguing-in-Publication Data
A catalogue record for this book is available from the British Library

Typeset by JS Typesetting Ltd, Portcawl, Mid Glamorgan
Printed and bound in the UK by 4edge Ltd, Essex

Contents

Foreword

Sara Cantillon and Diane Elson

The new *Gendered Economy* series of short books critically examines our understanding of the economy through the lens of gender. It showcases how economic relationships, actions and institutions are directly affected by gender norms and challenges many of the tenets that underpin both the mainstream and heterodox interpretation of how economies function. James Heinz's book *The Economy's Other Half* underscores this in its aim to challenge "the status quo of the current practice of macroeconomics by bringing gender into the way we understand how the economy works".

On the whole, neither mainstream nor heterodox macroeconomics, both in terms of theory development or policy formulation, pays attention to the role of gender in the economy and the implications of macro-level policies for gender equality. This book challenges that neglect. Starting from the premise that economies are shaped by gender relations and that macroeconomic policy is likely to affect every aspect of women's and men's economic lives, the book focuses on three specific areas of inquiry: firstly, how and why macroeconomic policies affect women and men differently, considering both fiscal policy (government spending, taxation and borrowing) and monetary policy (interventions that affect the money supply, interest rates and exchange rates); secondly, why the identification and measurement of the variables that form the basis of macroeconomics are incomplete and lead to poor policy choices; and thirdly, how investments in human beings, including unpaid and non-market care, affect the economy's prospects, and people's well-being, across generations.

Fiscal and monetary policies have large, broad-based effects on the economy influencing the level of demand, prices, employment, income distribution and productivity. Such policies, which fundamentally influence the productive capacity of the economy, are almost always designed and implemented without any specific reference to gender. It is usually presumed that macroeconomic formulation and policy advice is gender neutral because it does not explicitly target women and men. As this book shows, the difficulty with this conceptualization is that macroeconomic policies interact with structural features of the economy to produce distinct outcomes for women and men. Heintz demonstrates through detailed non-technical discussion of clear everyday examples, that macroeconomic policies are gender blind rather than gender neutral and, as such, raise the possibility of replicating and reinforcing existing inequalities between women and men. For instance, the public sector is often an important employer of women and its payroll represents a large component of overall government spending. Policies that reduce government spending – for example, in response to a high debt burden – will likely reduce the public payroll and this can have a disproportionately large effect on women's employment. In addition, cuts to availability of public services can increase women's unpaid work, because one possible coping mechanism is to increase the services produced with unpaid labour in the household – childcare, meal preparation and home maintenance, among others. For instance, cuts to medical services may mean that families with sick or disabled relatives must spend more time providing care within their own homes. Or consider the example of a government trying to support overall economic activity during a slump by engaging in large-scale investments in physical infrastructure. These investments may involve a large number of construction jobs, a sector dominated by men. If so, the economic stimulus would be biased in favour of men's employment.

Tax policies may also have different consequences for women and men. For instance, tax cuts for individuals with high incomes contain hidden gender biases. Because of inequalities in the labour market, women earn, on average, less than men, and the glass ceiling limits the number of women in high-paying professional jobs. Therefore, the benefits of proposed tax giveaways for the country's high earners will disproportionately accrue to men.

In the second section of the book Heintz focuses on the theme of mis-measurement and explores the issues of unpaid labour, care work, the limitations of GDP as a measure of either economic activity or well-being. Drawing on the work of feminist economists over the last 20 years he argues that taking into account non-market production is not only important for recognizing women's (and men's) unpaid work but could also fundamentally change how we think about macroeconomics. Heintz quotes results from time-use surveys in the United States which estimates the value of unpaid childcare for the US economy at $3.2 trillion in 2012, or approximately 20 per cent of that year's gross domestic product. This figure only captures unpaid childcare and does not include all the other non-market services produced within households. A 2018 International Labour Organization report, using survey data from 64 countries, estimated that the people performed over 16 billion hours of unpaid household work every day with women doing 76 per cent of this work. This means that women's unpaid labour in these countries totalled about 4.5 trillion hours a year, a volume of work equivalent to that of 2.1 billion full-time jobs.

Startling as these figures are Heintz succinctly argues that the macroeconomic implications of non-market household production are more far-reaching. Some of the most important aspects of non-market household production involve long-run investments that yield future returns. It takes time and resources to raise the next generation and the third section of the book takes on this challenge looking at investment in human beings, gender inequality and long-run economic performance.

Heintz argues that the realm of macroeconomics is generally content to ignore the fact that the human resources that run the economy are themselves "produced" and that the reproduction of society from one generation to the next represents a critical aspect of a sustainable economy. Social reproduction goes beyond simply ensuring that there are enough human bodies to constitute a future labour force. It requires substantial investment in human capacities that involve both market and non-market services. The investment produces real value that defies measurement solely in the metric of money and market exchange. A key point Heintz makes is the importance of social reproduction for the economy. Too often the argument is that more women must take on paid employment to generate economic growth, and unpaid work is seen only as an impediment to that growth. This misses the vital contribution to the economy that women (and to a lesser extent men) make in bringing up the next generation of workers. A reworked macroeconomics would recognize that goods and services are not the only things produced within an economic system. People, and their capacity to do things with their lives, are perhaps the most valuable creation of our economic system. The book concludes that we need to transform macroeconomics so that it recognizes this reality.

The Economy's Other Half makes the feminist economics critique of macroeconomic theory and policy accessible to a broad audience. It also breaks new ground in highlighting the contradiction between efforts to improve women's economic position and their bargaining power and the traditional ways in which social reproduction and investments in the next generation have been coordinated. Women may delay having children or forego childbearing altogether. More children may be raised by single mothers, and the costs of raising the next generation may become more unequally distributed, leading to unequal investments in children. All of these developments have potentially serious implications for the future trajectory of the economy and require new ways of coordinating the reproduction of the next generation in ways that are gender equitable.

This book demonstrates why economists and policy-makers must move from the inertia of gender-blind assumptions to take account of how gender structures economies in both the short and the long run; and how policies must change not only to address the current distribution of costs and benefits between women and men, but also to secure gender-equitable investment by households and government in sustaining the next generation.

Introduction

The US economy entered the twenty-first century exuberantly, with unemployment plunging to historic lows and families seeing the value of their assets grow to unimagined heights. A few years later, beginning in 2007, it all came crashing down. The US subprime mortgage crisis, which blossomed into a full-blown financial crisis a year later, made jobs evaporate and asset values disappear. On the employment front, men were hit hard, with unemployment rates reaching double digits. Women's employment fell, but not as far as men's. The press was quick to coin a new term to capture this economic assault on masculinity – the US was experiencing a "mancession". Despite the initial alarm, the mancession was relatively short-lived. By the beginning of 2010, men's employment already showed signs of recovery. Women weren't so lucky. Women's employment stagnated until almost a year and a half later, exhibiting signs of steady growth only in the second half of 2011.[1]

These kinds of macroeconomic meltdowns have happened elsewhere. Between 1998 and 2002, Argentina experienced one of the worst economic disasters in its history, earning this crisis the moniker of the "Argentine Great Depression". Unemployment reached record highs as Argentina's economy shrank by over 18 per cent. Despite the decline in employment opportunities, women's participation in the labour force actually rose modestly during the crisis (Montaño & Milosavljevic 2012). With formal jobs evaporating, employment in the informal sector

---

1. These trends are the author's description of employment estimates for the US civilian, non-institutional population from the US Bureau of Labor Statistics.

became an important coping strategy (Whitson 2007). During crises, like Argentina's, women's work allows families to make ends meet as they try to weather the economic storm. Economic distress may trigger reactions that hurt women in other ways. Due to macroeconomic policy choices, Zimbabwe experienced extreme rates of inflation beginning in the late 1990s that squeezed households and threatened living standards. Incidents of domestic violence rose as the country's economic crisis intensified (Masiyiwa 2017).

Economic crises are extreme events, yet they all illustrate an important lesson. Changes in the overall economic environment affect women and men differently. This holds true in non-crisis situations. Broad-based economic policies will have gender specific outcomes. We refer to these broad-based changes that influence the overall economic environment as macroeconomic factors. Some shifts in the macroeconomic environment arise through the complex dynamics of modern economies, but others are chosen. Macroeconomic policies represent interventions, undertaken by governments and central banks, that aim to shape the general economic environment. These policies are not specifically directed at men and women, yet they often have gender-specific impacts.

Why is this the case? Shifts in the macroeconomic environment, whether caused by shocks or deliberate policy choices, interact with structural features of the economy to produce distinct outcomes for women and men. For instance, in every economy worldwide, women are over-represented in certain occupations and sectors, and under-represented in others. Women are more likely to be employed as teachers and nurses than construction workers. The sectors of an economy respond differently to macroeconomic changes and, as a result, macro-level policies will have different effects on women's and men's employment.

Paid employment is only one channel through which gender inequalities interact with macroeconomic policies to produce distinct outcomes for men and women. There are other aspects of the economy where women and men occupy very different positions. Women tend to do, on average, more unpaid household work than men. The expected costs of raising children are frequently unequally distributed, with women bearing greater responsibility. Men frequently have more control over the use of income and decision-making within families. Social norms and formal laws often constrain the choices available to women, and women who step out of traditional gender roles may be subject to violence. All of these sources of gender inequality cause macroeconomics to affect women differently than men.

Not only do men and women occupy different positions in the economy, their economic contributions are treated differently. Commonly used macroeconomic indicators, such as gross domestic product (GDP), exclude, by design, much of the unpaid work that women do. Lots of time and money are spent raising the next generation, but standard macroeconomics fails to see this as a long-term investment. Because the variables at the heart of much of macroeconomics ignore many significant economic contributions by women, the policies formulated on the basis of these indicators contain hidden biases.

These neglected contributions are not trivial. The long-term health of the macroeconomy depends on the unpaid labour that women do. People do not spring into existence as fully-formed adults, ready to work. Children require a sizable investment of time to support their development into functioning adults. Without these investments in the next generation, the economy would eventually grind to a halt, with far-reaching consequences for everyone. Unpaid care work also contributes to overall well-being of adults, not simply children, particularly when they are sick or need assistance. Macroeconomics routinely assesses well-being in terms of average monetary income and the value of goods and services purchased. It fails to consider these other contributions. At best, this gives us a partial, flawed picture of how well the economy is doing.

The current practice of macroeconomics, be it in terms of developing theories or formulating policies, rarely takes these issues into account. This book aims to challenge this status quo and brings gender into the way we understand how the economy works. It begins with the question of distribution: how and why macroeconomic policies affect women and men differently. It considers two broad categories of macro policies:

fiscal policy, i.e. government spending, taxation and borrowing, and monetary policies, i.e. interventions that affect the money supply, interest rates and exchange rates. The book's second section then takes on the question of measurement, why the variables that form the conceptual foundation of modern macroeconomics are incomplete and may lead to poor policy choices. The final section takes a long-run view. It considers how investments in human beings, including unpaid and non-market care, affect the economy's prospects, and people's well-being, across generations.

The argument throughout is simple: if we really want to take gender seriously, we need to transform the way we think about macroeconomics.

1

Gender inequality and macroeconomic policy

MACROECONOMIC POLICY AND GENDER INEQUALITY: WHAT ARE THE CONNECTIONS?

Macroeconomics claims as its domain the policies, prices and practices that affect the economy as a whole. In contrast, microeconomics primarily concerns itself with the choices individuals and businesses make. In many respects, this way of carving up the economy is artificial. Macro–micro overlaps are commonplace. Individual decisions and behaviours, taken together, affect the overall economy. Likewise, a general collapse of financial markets changes the choices people make. There are certain interventions that have broad-based impacts and have the potential to alter the general economic environment. We call these interventions macroeconomic policies.

Macroeconomic policies are typically divided into two categories: fiscal policies and monetary policies. Fiscal policies are concerned with how governments mobilize resources and how they spend the money they have. They include government spending, tax policy, and the generation of other types of public revenues. Governments are also capable of borrowing when expenditures exceed current revenues. Fiscal policies are therefore concerned with deficit financing and the management of the public debt.

Monetary policies are the remit of central banks. They affect the supply of credit and the resources available to financial institutions. They are able to influence some of the most important prices in the economy: interest rates and exchange rates. Interest rates affect the cost of borrowing and impact major economic decisions: whether to buy a house, whether to expand a business, and whether to take out a loan for a new car. Exchange rates have a huge effect on international transactions. They influence a country's ability to compete on global markets and the cost of imported essentials, such as food and energy.

Governments and central banks implement macroeconomic policies with a number of objectives in mind. In some cases, macroeconomic policies attempt to promote economic growth. They can be used to try to insure that there is adequate demand for the goods and services an economy produces. By changing the level of demand, they have a knock-on effect on the level of employment. Because of this, one common macroeconomic policy objective is to reduce unemployment. But macroeconomic policy-makers are also concerned about prices. Reckless macroeconomic management may lead to high rates of inflation that erode living standards. Controlling inflation is frequently a central macroeconomic objective.

Macroeconomic policies work through a number of channels. One important channel is aggregate demand – the overall demand for goods and services exchanged in markets. Fiscal policies alter aggregate demand directly. Since the government is such a big player in the economy, changes in government spending affect the general level of demand. However, such spending has to be financed, most commonly through taxation. Higher taxes reduce the resources available to households and businesses and dampen demand. Because spending and taxes work in opposite directions, the impact of tax-financed public spending on overall demand may be ambiguous. But governments have another option. They can borrow to finance additional spending without raising taxes. Fiscal policies aimed at boosting demand therefore tend to rely on debt-financed expenditures.

Monetary policies also affect the overall purchasing power in the economy. They do this by influencing the resources available to financial institutions that make loans and extend credit, such as commercial banks. When the supply of credit increases, households and businesses find it easier and cheaper to borrow to finance a broad range of purchases – from new equipment to new houses. As long as people are willing to borrow and banks are able to lend, an expansion of credit will support more aggregate demand in the economy.

Fiscal policy involves the allocation of public funds to different areas of spending in the budget. It therefore determines which public goods and services will be produced and how much will be provided. For instance, fiscal policy will affect spending on education and the delivery of educational services. Education represents an investment in human beings that has a long-run impact on the productive potential of the economy. Governments also redistribute resources through fiscal policy. Households and businesses transfer money to the government in the form of taxes, and governments, in turn, transfer money to households and businesses. Low-income households may receive grants to reduce the prevalence of poverty and businesses may receive subsidies to promote certain types of investment.

Monetary and fiscal policies influence the productive capacity of the economy. Public investment in infrastructure, such as water, sanitation, electricity and roads, provides economic benefits to the population and to businesses. Through its influence on interest rates, monetary policy can encourage or discourage investment. High interest rates make it costly to borrow to expand business activity, while lower rates will tend to encourage productive investment.

Fiscal policy is typically set by specific agencies within the government, usually a Ministry of Finance or the Treasury. Budgets and tax policy are often subject to parliamentary or congressional approval. In contrast, central banks have been set up to conduct monetary policy. Central banks are typically statutory institutions, established by governments, to oversee the banking system and the money supply. Most central banks worldwide have some degree of independence from the government. Their independent status theoretically creates a barrier between the political machinations of the government and the implementation of monetary policy. The formulation of macroeconomic policy, both fiscal and monetary, is typically conducted as a technocratic exercise, with limited participation and varying degrees of transparency. This limits the direct engagement of a country's citizenship with these areas of economic policy-making.

From this brief overview, we see that fiscal and monetary policies have large, broad-based effects on the economy as a whole. They influence the level of demand, prices, employment, productivity and the distribution of income. Macroeconomic policies are usually designed and implemented without any specific reference to gender. Because of this, it is often said that macroeconomic policies are "gender blind". For instance, when central banks raise interest rates, perhaps in an effort to bring down inflation, they do not differentiate between men and women with respect to the policy instrument (i.e. the interest rate) or the policy objective (i.e. lower inflation). Since the conduct of macro policies is gender blind, little attention is paid to the different ways these policies affect men and women.

But gender blind does not mean gender neutral. Macroeconomic policies interact with structural features of the economy, such as the distribution of unpaid work and the segregation of men and women into different types of employment, to produce distinct outcomes for women and men (Rubery 2014). This raises the possibility that gender-blind macroeconomic policies will replicate and reinforce existing inequalities between women and men.

Take the example of labour market segregation, in which women are over-represented in some types of paid work (e.g. garment workers) and under-represented in others (e.g. taxi drivers). Different sectors of the economy, and different occupations, may be more sensitive to macroeconomic policies than others. For instance, the public sector is often an important employer of women in professional service jobs, such as teachers and nurses. The wages and salaries of government workers represent large components of overall government spending. Policies that reduce government spending – for example, in response to a high debt burden – will likely reduce the public payroll and this can have a disproportionately large effect on women's employment. Or consider the example of a government trying to support overall economic activity during a slump by engaging in large-scale investments in physical infrastructure. These investments may involve a large number of construction jobs, a sector dominated by men. If so, the economic stimulus would be biased in favour of men's employment.

Women and men may also have different experiences when the macroeconomic environment changes because of different responsibilities for unpaid household work. Budget cuts, restrictive credit policies, and higher interest rates will reduce demand in the economy, potentially leading to a fall in household resources when unemployment rises and incomes are squeezed (Berik & Kongar 2015). Households also utilize public services directly. If these services are reduced, families will need to adjust. One possible coping mechanism is to increase the services produced with unpaid labour in the household – childcare, meal preparation, and home maintenance, among others. For instance, cuts to medical services may mean that families with sick or disabled relatives must spend more time providing care within their own homes.

Since women perform more unpaid household work than men, the weight of adjustment will likely fall on their shoulders. In some cases, women will simply work longer hours. Increased demand for unpaid work can also constrain women's ability to engage in paid employment. Because of the gender division of labour within the household, women and men experience economic contractions differently.

Households are not homogenous. Many have children, others do not. In some households, there are two or more people of working age, while in others a single adult takes on the responsibility of keeping things afloat. Macroeconomic shocks have different implications for different households. Children are less able to contribute to maintaining the family, they require both time and money, and therefore they tend to consume more than they produce. An economic downturn will, on average, have a more significant negative effect on families with children than on other households. When a household has two or more adults, they are more resilient when it comes to withstanding a shock because the adults are able to pool resources to manage risks. Consider two families – one with two adults, both of whom work in paid employment, and the second with only one adult. The loss of a job will be less devastating to the two-earner family compared to the family with only one adult in a paid job.

Families with children maintained by single adult women face multiple risks that leave them particularly vulnerable. The presence of children raises the costs of sustaining the household. Moreover, if the single mother does not have friends or relatives that can help out, she must be "on call" if her children get sick or need additional care. This limits her job choices. The fact that there is only one adult earner means that total household income is, on average, lower than in comparable two-earner households and, for the reasons discussed above, a single-mother family faces higher risks from economic shocks. Due to labour market segregation and outright discrimination, women earn less than men, further lowering the resources available. Child support (or child maintenance) can help, but not all mothers receive payments from the fathers of their children. Taken together, it's not surprising that changes at the macroeconomic level will affect some households more than others, and these asymmetric consequences are gendered.

FISCAL POLICY AND GENDER INEQUALITY

When we consider how fiscal policy affects gender equality, budgets are of foremost importance. The government's budget represents a plan of how much will be spent on what, and how the government will pay for it all. Budgetary decisions affect the allocation of public expenditures and reflect government priorities. The state may cut support for the poor in favour of military spending, or reduce foreign aid in order to invest more at home. The allocation of public spending among competing uses has a direct effect on gender equality because changes in government expenditure affect women's lives differently than men's.

Consider the findings of a study that examined the effects of changes in government healthcare spending on maternal mortality rates in 24 European Union countries over the period 1981–2010. Maternal mortality is a leading cause of death for women in their 20s and 30s in many countries. Government expenditures are an important source of healthcare financing and can improve access to services that reduce the risk of women dying during pregnancy, childbirth and shortly after delivery.[1]

---

1. In the study described here, maternal mortality is defined as death during pregnancy, childbirth, or within 42 days after delivery.

The research found that a 1 per cent decline in government health spending was associated with a more than 10 per cent increase in maternal mortality (Maruthappu *et al.* 2014). This indicates that changes in a general category of expenditure, such as health spending, can have gender-specific effects.

Spending on basic infrastructure provides another example of how public spending affects women and men differently. In many low-income countries, women spend a significant amount of time collecting and carrying water. Access to a water tap can transform women's lives by dramatically cutting the time needed to supply water to their households. Decisions regarding the allocation of funds to basic infrastructure projects, specifically access to water and sanitation facilities, will affect women's daily lives differently than men's (Bibler & Zuckerman 2013).

This is not to say that cuts to government health expenditures will have little effect on men's overall health status. Or that men do not benefit from access to basic water and sanitation facilities. Budget cuts are not automatically biased against women; men can be hurt as well. However, the critical point to recognize is that changes to budget allocations will affect women and men differently, and we have no way of knowing about these impacts unless these distributive dynamics are specifically analyzed and taken into account when formulating fiscal policies.

Government budgets represent the one area of macroeconomics in which significant inroads have been made with regard to documenting the effects of fiscal policy choices on women and men (Elson 1998). This type of analysis is carried out using an approach called "gender responsive budgeting". Gender responsive budgeting assesses the impact of budget choices on women and men. It involves analyzing the allocation of public spending, the effects of tax policy, and the beneficiaries of public service delivery and public investments to identify gender-specific impacts of fiscal policy. Gender responsive budgeting is now a widely recognized approach to evaluate the implementation of government commitments for improving gender equality and closing outcome gaps between women and men.

A 2016 assessment of gender responsive budgeting initiatives by the International Monetary Fund found that, at the time, over 80 countries around the world had undertaken some form of gender assessment with regard to budget policies (Stotsky 2016). One step in analyzing budgets from a gender perspective involves examining the allocation of public spending and the direct effect this may have on women and girls relative to men and boys. For instance, are educational expenditures distributed in such a way as to support girls' educational attainment to the same extent as boys'? Looking at the allocation of spending is critical, but ideally, gender responsive budgeting should go further. It should not only analyze how the money is divided, but also look at the actual delivery of public services and investments and who benefits from them.

Let's return to the case of public health expenditures by way of example. Imagine that we are analyzing proposed cuts to health expenditures. We would want to analyze which areas of spending would be cut and what the gender specific consequences may be. Will the cuts mean large lay-offs of nurses who are disproportionately women? Will spending on prenatal and postnatal care be reduced? But we should not stop there. We would also want to know to what extent the spending cuts threaten actual service delivery and who bears the burden of adjusting to a curtailed supply of public services and investments. Suppose lower expenditures result in the early discharge of patients from public hospitals. These patients, when they return home, will likely require care from family members – care they would have received in the hospital. A likely scenario is that female family members will take on this additional care work. This is a real cost to the women involved and an important consequence of budget decisions. Gender responsive budgeting, to the extent possible, should take these outcomes into consideration.

Spending is not the only aspect of fiscal policy that matters. Taxes are also important. Although many approaches to gender responsive budgeting focus exclusively on public expenditures, tax policy may also have different consequences for women and men (Grown & Valodia 2010). Consider the work of the Women's Budget Group, based in the UK and established, following the 2008 financial crisis, to analyze the gender specific consequences of Britain's fiscal policy, particularly the austerity policies that were proposed in the wake of the crisis. The Women's Budget Group has pointed out that tax cuts for individuals with high incomes contain hidden gender biases.[2] Because of inequalities in the labour market, women earn, on average, less than men, and the glass ceiling limits the number of women in high-paying professional jobs. Therefore, the benefits of proposed tax giveaways for the country's high earners will disproportionately accrue to men. This could further widen the after-tax earnings gap between men and women.

Government spending must be financed somehow and taxes provide a major source of revenues. But increasing taxes to finance higher spending has an ambiguous effect on overall demand in the economy. This is because, while direct government purchases raise demand for goods and services, higher taxes leave households with less disposable income to spend and businesses with smaller surpluses to invest. Less household consumption and lower business investment reduce total demand. If the goal of fiscal policy is to boost aggregate demand, for example – to try to reduce unemployment, governments should borrow to finance additional spending.

An expansion of overall demand in the economy is not gender neutral, for reasons already discussed. One contributing factor is that some sectors are more sensitive to changes in aggregate demand than others. There are some purchases, including investments in expanding productive capacity, that increase significantly during good times, but fall rapidly when the economy experiences hard times. Other categories of demand are more recession-proof, such as necessities that are needed in bad times as well as good times. Because women's employment is segregated, with women more likely to work in some sectors relative to others, an expansion of demand will have different effects on women's and men's employment.

But there are other reasons to pay attention to debt-financed expansions of government expenditure. The public debt must be serviced and the cost of servicing the debt, in terms of interest payments and repaying what was borrowed, represent an on-going claim on government expenditures. As debt payments increase, all else being equal, fewer

---

2. https://wbg.org.uk/wp-content/uploads/2017/11/taxation-pre-Budget-nov-2017-final.pdf (accessed 29 October 2018).

resources are available to finance other areas of spending. If the debt servicing payments become too great, the government will be unable to meet its current obligations, triggering a fiscal crisis.

The situation is more complicated when governments borrow from abroad. Foreign debt tends to be denominated in a major international currency, such as the US dollar or the euro. Because of this debt service payments must be made in a similar "hard" currency. Foreign debt becomes unsustainable when debtor countries run out of the reserves of foreign currency needed to service the debt. Again, an inability to service the debt triggers a fiscal crisis.

Power dynamics also come into play. In credit markets, the creditors typically represent the short-side of the market, since they control access to credit and the demand for loans frequently outstrips the supply. The threat of withholding access to financial resources, and the ability to demand repayment on specified terms, gives lenders power over borrowers (Bowles & Gintis 1993). Debt operates as a disciplinary device that can be used to shape government policy, reinforce global dependencies and restructure economies.

So, what happens when a country runs into a fiscal crisis? Countries experiencing a fiscal crisis typically end up being bailed out and required to restructure their debt to make repayment possible. Countries may borrow from international financial institutions like the International Monetary Fund (IMF) that act as lenders of last resort. As part of the bailout and restructuring process, creditors often impose policy conditionalities aimed at insuring that future debt servicing payments will be forthcoming.[3] For instance, governments might be required to limit debt-financed expenditures and to cut spending to insure that they have the space in their budgets to service their debts. They might also be required to adopt strategies in an effort to boost exports, which would, if successful, increase earnings of the foreign exchange needed to pay back loans from abroad.

---

3. In the 1980s and 1990s, the conditionalities that international financial institutions, such as the International Monetary Fund and the World Bank, demanded were often packaged as "structural adjustment programs". Gender analyses of these programs can be found in Elson (1995) and Benería (1995).

The world saw these dynamics of debt, power and adjustment play out with the sovereign debt crisis in Europe that emerged following the 2008 meltdown in global financial markets. The European sovereign debt crisis was a result of the inability of smaller eurozone countries to service their public debt – specifically, Greece, Ireland and Portugal. Rising debt-servicing costs created a situation in which public debt in these countries was no longer sustainable (Blundell-Wignall & Slovik 2011). The situation was exacerbated when credit ratings agencies downgraded their risk assessments for the public debt in the affected countries, contributing to higher costs of borrowing.

The financial sectors of European countries held large amounts of this sovereign debt, and the sector's stability was directly threatened by the possibility of default. For these reasons, rescue packages were organized to stabilize the situation (Zandstra 2011).[4] The rescue packages included emergency loans and agreements to restructure the debts to make the debt-servicing payments affordable. The rescue packages included conditionalities requiring large cuts to government spending. The cost of the macroeconomic adjustments adopted to respond to the crisis was therefore borne by the populations of the countries introducing austerity programmes.

As discussed earlier, changes in government spending, such as those associated with austerity programmes, have gender specific effects. The case of Greece is illustrative. The sovereign debt crisis was devastating for Greece with both GDP and employment falling around 20 per cent between 2008 and 2012 (Karamessini 2014). The crisis in Greece caused massive job losses for both men and women, with men experiencing particularly rapid increases in unemployment. As households incomes were squeezed, more women entered the labour force looking for jobs – although there were not many jobs to be had (*Ibid.*). As part of the deal with the IMF and other eurozone countries, Greece agreed, in 2010, to implement an "Economic Adjustment Plan" (EAP) that required sharp cuts to government spending, involving reductions in salaries and overall

---

4. Two stability mechanisms were used to administer the rescue programs: the European Financial Stability Mechanism and, when more substantial interventions were required, the European Financial Stability Facility.

levels of public employment. Women's public sector employment fell somewhat more rapidly than men's after the adoption of the EAP, welfare services – including childcare – were cut, and the minimum age of retirement for women, which was lower than for men prior to the crisis, was increased substantially in order to contain spending on public pensions (*Ibid.*). The full impact of the sovereign debt crisis and austerity budgets on women and men in Greece will not be know for many years to come, but the crisis illustrates how macroeconomic shocks and policy responses can have gender specific effects.

There is another way fiscal policy affects gender equality. As discussed earlier, macroeconomic policies have gender specific outcomes because they interact with existing structural sources of gender inequality. One way of addressing these structural inequalities is to change the features of the economy that perpetuate gender inequality, such as occupation segregation or the unequal burden of unpaid work. Such changes are not simple and require committed interventions. They also require resources. When fiscal resources are squeezed, the ability to pursue policies that address the underlying causes of gender inequality is compromised. Fiscal policy defines the resource envelope within which governments must operate. Restrictive fiscal stances prevent the mobilization of the resources needed to finance interventions that support gender equality or to insure that government spending and taxation have positive, rather than negative, distributive consequences.

MONETARY POLICY, FINANCE AND GENDER INEQUALITY

Thanks to approaches such as gender responsive budgeting, the distributive effects of fiscal policies are increasingly recognized and understood. Far less attention is paid to the consequences for women and men of other types of macroeconomic policies. Specifically, the gender specific effects of monetary policies are rarely considered. However, for reasons already discussed, monetary policies affect women and men differently through their influence over aggregate demand, the supply of credit, interest rates and exchange rates.

Pretty much all central banks around the world have one policy goal that trumps all others: price stability. Price stability is typically interpreted as maintaining very low rates of inflation, usually well below 5 per cent a year. High rates of inflation can be costly. When prices increase rapidly, and particularly when they grow unexpectedly, it becomes hard to conduct predictable economic transactions. How much should wages and salaries be adjusted to reflect cost of living increases? How can loan contracts accurately capture changes in purchasing power caused by rising prices? For people on fixed incomes, that is – incomes whose monetary values do not change over time – high inflation reduces the amount those incomes can buy and causes living standards to fall. If inflation spins out of control and reaches extreme levels, such as 500 per cent or 1,000 per cent (a situation referred to as hyperinflation), holding money for even a short period is costly, since purchasing power falls quickly.

If there were no trade-offs, everyone would want to keep inflation close to zero. But there is a problem. Keeping inflation at very low levels may require sacrifices elsewhere in the economy. Efforts to lower inflation through monetary policies require constricting the growth of the money supply to keep demand from pushing up prices. But efforts to restrain demand slow growth and limit job creation. Trying to push inflation towards zero through monetary policy can come at the cost of less output sold, lower incomes and higher rates of unemployment. For these reasons, some central banks have a secondary goal: to manage the overall level of demand in the economy, consistent with stable rates of inflation, in order to moderate downturns and forestall excessive unemployment.

Although monetary policy can be used to promote growth and job creation, most central banks, in their routine policy deliberations, focus almost exclusively on lowering inflation (Epstein & Yeldan 2008). In order to achieve their inflation targets, central banks have a number of strategies at their disposal. Central banks are able to adjust parameters set for the private banking sector that influence how much commercial banks are able to lend. They do this by raising or lowering the amount of lendable reserves in the banking system through interventions such as changing the reserve requirement, adjusting the discount rate, or, most commonly, by buying or selling financial assets. Reserves represent the cash that banks have on hand. Banks are able to lend out any reserves they have beyond a minimum level they are required to keep (i.e. the reserve requirement). By changing the lendable reserves available, central banks affect the capacity of the banks to lend money.

One possible target of monetary policy is the growth rate of credit and the overall money supply. Central banks could set a target for how fast the money supply or available credit grows and then use the tools at their disposal to meet that goal. However, money supply targets have limitations. While central banks can influence the supply of money or credit, they have far less influence over the demand for money. Because of this, many central banks prefer to use an interest rate target. Interest rates reflect the influence of both demand and supply conditions. Central banks use their ability to influence the supply of credit to affect interest rates. If the central bank restricts the supply of credit relative to demand, the price people are willing to pay for loans (i.e. the interest rate) rises. If the central bank wants to target a lower interest rate, it allows the credit supply to increase faster than demand.

A common approach to monetary policy is to use interest rates to try to meet an inflation target. If the central bank decides inflation is too high, it can raise interest rates by restricting how fast the credit supply grows relative to demand. Less credit and higher interest rates reduce demand and purchasing power in the economy. If the central bank believes demand is too low and inflation is under control, it might lower interest rates by increasing the growth rate of credit relative to demand. Expanding the money supply lifts up aggregate demand.

Central banks also have a role in influencing exchange rates. In globally integrated economies, changes in the exchange rate affect prices and inflation. Imagine a country that, because of a lack of domestic production, depends on critical imports such as food, fuel, steel, or equipment purchased from abroad. Or a country whose domestic producers primarily compete with imports from other countries. If exchange rates were to depreciate, so that the domestic currency weakened against other currencies, the price of imports would rise. This could raise prices generally because of the effect of the depreciation on the cost of key imports. It would also allow domestic producers, whose primary competition is producers in other countries, to raise prices. In both cases, a depreciation triggers inflation.

Central banks are able to intervene in the market for foreign exchange in order to influence the domestic exchange rate. By buying and selling foreign exchange, such as US dollars, a central bank can cause the domestic currency to appreciate (increase in value) or depreciate (decrease in value). These changes in the exchange rate will affect the domestic price level. The degree to which changes in exchange rates are passed on as changes in domestic prices depends on the structure of the economy. The prices in import-dependent countries and in countries with concentrated industries that primarily compete with foreign companies will tend to be more responsive to changes in exchange rates than in countries with different economic structures.

If a central bank is concerned about inflation, it will tend to restrict the supply of credit and raise interest rates. It may also try to prevent a depreciation of the currency. Anti-inflation policies are typically associated with higher interest rates, an appreciation of the exchange rate, and tighter control over aggregate demand. While these policies could be called gender-blind, their impacts are not gender neutral.

Why might monetary policy have gender-specific effects? As with fiscal policy, monetary policy changes the macroeconomic environment and interacts with structural features of the economy to produce different outcomes for women and men. Consider the gender segregation of labour markets, with women's and men's employment concentrated in different sectors and occupations. Each sector of the economy will have a distinct reaction to changes in monetary policies. Some sectors are more demand-sensitive than others. Some react more strongly to rising interest rates. Some have greater exposure to international trade, which makes the movements in exchange rates particularly important.

For instance, in some countries, women are concentrated in labour-intensive manufacturing operations, such as garment production or the assembly of electronic products. A depreciation of the domestic exchange rate makes these sectors more competitive, since exports become cheaper in global markets and the domestic price of imports rises. This could have a positive impact on women's employment. Conversely, an appreciation of the exchange rate, which may be associated with vigorous anti-inflation policies, would reduce employment in these sectors.

The unequal distribution of the burden of unpaid care work can also produce uneven responses to monetary policies. Contractionary monetary policy, used to fight inflation, limits aggregate demand and may lead to slower income growth and higher unemployment. This squeezes household resources and families must adjust. One strategy to cope with macroeconomic changes that negatively affect household income is to substitute away from goods and services purchased in the market and turn to goods and services produced with unpaid labour at home. Since women typically perform more unpaid labour than men, women may bear a larger share of these household-level costs of adjustment to macroeconomic changes.

These arguments are mostly speculative. We currently know far less about the gender-specific effects of monetary policy than we do about fiscal policy. No real equivalent to gender responsive budgeting has been deployed in countries around the world to evaluate the policy choices of central banks with regard to their impact on women and men. The few studies that have examined the possibility of gender-specific outcomes of monetary policy changes have focused on employment and labour market outcomes. This is largely because there is more data on labour market outcomes and changes in employment are easier to track over time. Linking monetary policy changes to shifts in intra-household dynamics, such as the distribution of unpaid labour, is more challenging.

One early study looked at episodes of inflation reduction characterized by restrictive monetary stances, measured by increases in interest rates, in a range of developing countries. It found that these episodes of inflation reduction associated with higher interest rates are likely to be correlated with slower growth of women's employment relative to men's, when compared to long-run employment trends (Braunstein & Heintz 2008). Examples of countries examined include Brazil, Colombia, Costa Rica, India, Philippines and the Republic of Korea. The inequalities in employment outcomes were less evident when monetary policy was less restrictive. The study also found that differences in the dynamics of women's and men's employment are less pronounced when exchange rates do not appreciate, suggesting that interest rates and exchange rates have gender-specific effects.

However, not all studies reach the same conclusion. Research on monetary policy among the relatively higher income countries in the Organization for Economic Co-operation and Development (OECD) countries found no evidence of different effects on women's and men's unemployment rates (Tachtamanova & Sierminska 2009). The gender effects of monetary policy are not uniform and appear to vary with different economic and social structures. Research on Federal Reserve policy in the United States found evidence that higher policy interest rates have a stronger negative effect on women's unemployment relative to men's, but this relationship varies from state to state and changes with the racial composition of the population (Seguino & Heintz 2012).

To more fully understand the gender effects of monetary policy, an approach that parallels gender responsive budgeting is needed. There is no reason why a gender responsive approach to monetary policy could not be adopted and the distinct effects of monetary policy on women and men taken into account. Currently, data limitations would prevent in-depth analysis of all facets of potential gender bias in all cases. However, central banks could undertake initial assessments of the gender effects of monetary policy. As data availability, quality and frequency improve, so too would the quality of the gender impact analysis.

The regulation of financial markets, financial institutions and financial flows is another policy area closely related to monetary policy. One goal of such regulations is to reduce economic volatility and prevent crises, such as the 2008 global financial crisis. Governments can adopt various measures to promote economic stability. For instance, capital controls are regulations on financial movements into and out of a country. They can reduce the probability that a country will experience a sizeable outflow of financial resources that can trigger a crisis (Chang & Grabel 2014). A range of countries have used these kinds of policies in an attempt to reduce volatility, including Brazil, China, Colombia, Chile, India and Malaysia (Cordero & Montecino 2010).

Other financial regulations are targeted at domestic financial institutions and markets. These policies are sometimes called "macro-prudential policies" and they aim to prevent the financial system from becoming dangerously fragile (IMF 2013; Lim *et al.* 2011). A central concern of these regulations is to prevent the economy from becoming over-leveraged. This occurs when debt, both public and private, expands more rapidly than the income and assets that are used to back or repay the debt. Examples of macro-prudential regulations include making the capital requirements of banks dependent on economic conditions, so that capital requirements increase when credit expands too rapidly; requiring that the assets of financial institutions be linked to their equity; and limiting debt-financed acquisition of financial assets.

Why is financial instability a gender issue? Women and men have different degrees of economic vulnerability and the burden of adjusting to economic crises will not be identical. The introduction to this book provided several examples of these differences – in terms of unemployment, labour force participation, and the incidence of domestic violence. Just like certain fiscal and monetary policies, economic crises squeeze resources and households must adapt. When women and men have different roles in the household, their responses to a macroeconomic crisis will also differ. Depending on these responses, the burden of adjustment may fall more heavily on the shoulders of women and existing gender inequalities may become entrenched. More generally, as with other changes to the macroeconomic environment, economic crises will have distinct effects on women and men.

Financial crises reduce the resources available to governments and may affect the relative size of the public debt. In some cases, governments respond to a crisis by pursuing counter-cyclical policies – borrowing to shore up public spending when many other sectors of the economy are contracting. However, a common response to economic crises is austerity, cutting government spending so as to live within a country's reduced means. As discussed earlier, depending on how the cuts are made, austerity policies may have gender-specific outcomes. For these reasons, macroeconomic policies that aim to regulate financial markets and reduce the likelihood of economic crises have the potential to make a positive contribution to gender equality.

DOES ECONOMIC GROWTH REDUCE GENDER INEQUALITY?

Macroeconomic policies have gender-specific effects that affect inequalities between women and men. But what macroeconomic policy should be adopted if the aim is to improve gender equality? Let's consider one of the simplest answers to this question. Using fairly crude cross-country comparisons, there appears to be a positive relationship between many indicators of gender equality, such as the ratio of school enrollment for boys and girls or women's labour force participation relative to men's, and average GDP per person (UN Women 2015). These relationships are not perfect. Countries with similar levels of GDP per capita may have very different outcomes when it comes to gender equality, and this positive relationship may not hold over the full range, from the lowest GDP per capita to the highest. Nevertheless, for a number of important indicators, higher GDP is, in general terms, correlated with certain measurements of gender equality.

This suggests that economic growth, defined traditionally as sustained increases in GDP, is associated with better outcomes with respect to gender equality. If we accept this premise, the problem of how to design macroeconomic policies to promote gender equality is simple. There is no need to delve into the details of the distributive consequences of policy decisions for women and men. The various issues discussed in the previous sections, while interesting, can be set aside. All that is needed is to develop a set of macroeconomic policies that will maximize growth, and gender equality will take care of itself.

Although this line of reasoning is attractive, things are not so simple. For instance, growth that is based on maintaining competitiveness in global markets can actually reinforce gender inequalities. When there is a pay gap between women and men, with women paid less than men for equivalent work, women become an inexpensive source of labour (Seguino 2000). Narrowing the pay gap by raising women's wages could compromise growth based on the availability of cheap paid labour. There is no reason to believe that faster growth, in itself, will automatically close the gap.

There are areas in which a move towards gender equality has been shown to be correlated with either higher income per capita or faster growth. For example, a narrower gap in education attainment between men/boys and women/girls appears to have a positive impact on average incomes (e.g. Klasen & Lamanna 2009; Dollar & Gatti 1999). Women who work in paid employment are often concentrated in jobs considered "women's work" where productivity and earnings are low. These patterns of segregation indicate an inefficient allocation of labour in the sense that women are prevented from participating in activities where they would be more productive (Tzannotos 1999). Reducing the degree of gender segregation in labour markets should contribute to higher productivity for the economy as a whole. But in these cases, the direction of causality appears to be reversed. Less gender inequality leads to higher growth rather than the other way around.

The unpaid work that women do is both a fundamental source of gender inequality and a potential subsidy to economic growth. For instance, the welfare arrangements under South Korea's development strategy from the 1960s to the early 1990s, a period of rapid growth and economic development, depended on households to provide care services rather than on government programmes financed by taxation. This arrangement was based on a highly gendered division of labour, in which women performed most of the unpaid care work (Peng 2012). If these services were publicly provided and financed through taxes, including business taxes, the costs of doing business in Korea would have been higher and growth might have been compromised.

Although many recognize that per capita GDP and many measures of gender equality are positively correlated, the relationship is much more complex. At best, the evidence that growth will automatically bring about greater gender equality is mixed (Kabeer & Natali 2013; Duflo 2012). There is no reason to believe that macroeconomic policies that focus exclusively on growth will deliver improvements in gender equality. If we care about persistent inequalities between women and men, a different approach to macroeconomics is needed.

TOWARDS A GENDER RESPONSIVE MACROECONOMICS

If growth is not enough to address gender inequalities, then we need to be more cognizant of the different effects macroeconomic policies and shocks have on women and men. Gender responsive budgeting represents an important step in this direction. The same approach could be expanded and applied to all areas of macroeconomic policy-making, including monetary and financial policies. This would involve conducting gender impact analyses to consider the distributive consequences of policy choices on gender equality.

Having said this, its important to recognize that macroeconomic policies are no magic wand. They are fairly blunt instruments that affect the overall economic environment. They impact on women and men differently because they interact with structural features of the economy that perpetuate gender inequalities. Altering macroeconomic policy choices cannot, by themselves, address the underlying sources of gender inequality. Macroeconomic policies need to be coordinated with other interventions that would move our economies onto a path towards greater gender equality.

2

The mis-measured economy: incorporating feminist ideas into macroeconomic accounting

Women do an enormous amount of unpaid labour. A 2018 report of the International Labour Organization (ILO) took survey data from 64 countries, representing two-thirds of the world's population, and estimated that the people in the countries surveyed performed over 16 billion hours of unpaid household work *everyday* (ILO 2018). Women did 76 per cent of this work. This means that women's unpaid labour in these countries totaled about 4.5 trillion hours a year, a volume of work equivalent to that of 2.1 billion full-time jobs (based on a 40-hour paid working week).[1]

What is all this work worth? Estimates for the US economy of the value of unpaid childcare, an important component of non-market household production, run to trillions of dollars – one calculation for 2012 places it at $3.2 trillion, or approximately 20 per cent of that year's GDP (Suh & Folbre 2014). This number only captures unpaid childcare, and does not add in all the other non-market services produced within households. Efforts at valuing unpaid work across a variety of countries typically come up with estimates in the range of 15–40 per cent of GDP, depending on the methods used (UN Women 2015). This range of the

---

1. The statistics reported here correspond to "unpaid care work", defined as unpaid work carried out to sustain the well-being and maintenance of others in a household or a community. It includes the direct care of people and indirect caring services, such as meal preparation or routine housework. It excludes the household production of goods for own-use, including fetching water or fuel.

estimated value of unpaid work is of the same order of magnitude as the monetary value of the public sector's contribution to the measured economy. Macroeconomists would never think to exclude the government from their analysis. Yet non-market production using unpaid labour is routinely ignored in macroeconomic statistics.

Earlier we argued that changes in the macroeconomic environment interact with structural sources of gender inequality to yield different outcomes for women and men. One source of inequality is women's disproportionate burden of unpaid household work. The unbalanced way in which women's labour is allocated must be addressed to reduce, and ideally eliminate, persistent gender inequalities in the world's economies. But it is hard to rebalance the non-market side of the economy when unpaid work does not count and is rarely acknowledged.

Feminist economists have long pointed out the need to recognize, value, and do something about the unequal burden of unpaid work. But why is unpaid work missing from most reckonings of the size of the macroeconomy? To understand the arbitrary exclusion of unpaid work, it helps to take a brief look at the history of macroeconomic measurement. The official accounting system used to size up economic activity at the macro level – the amount produced, saved, invested and consumed – is relatively new. The national accounts currently used to measure the US economy only date back to the 1940s (BEA 2017). The first international standards for measuring the macroeconomy, called the System of National Accounts (SNA), were introduced in 1953.

There were earlier efforts to try to estimate aggregate economic activity. Back in the seventeenth century, Sir William Petty was one of the first to calculate a national income and he published estimates for England at the time. But national accounting was slow to take off. By the beginning of the twentieth century, national income estimates had only been developed for nine countries – produced at non-regular intervals and employing a variety of techniques (Bos 1992). With the founding of the Soviet Union in 1917, national income accounting took on a practical urgency. Centrally planned economies required aggregate measurements to allow governments to make decisions about how to run the economy. Shortly afterwards, the Great Depression engulfed much of the capitalist world, and spurred on efforts to understand its causes in order to prevent a reoccurrence. Because of the Great Depression, the League of Nations pushed countries to develop comparable national economic statistics (BEA 2017). Thinkers like John Maynard Keynes, among others, developed new ways of analyzing what makes economies tick, giving birth to the discipline of macroeconomics. If the behaviour of aggregate production, spending, and investment governed a country's economic fate, then measurements of these macroeconomic concepts were needed to steer the economy on a path to prosperity and to avoid collapse.

Much of the work that was done on macroeconomic measurement in the 1930s came together as the System of National Accounts we know today. It is important to recognize that, despite all the hard work and intelligence that went into their development, the System of National Accounts remains a human invention based on what the men who worked on this national accounting system at that time believed was important to measure.[2]

An example helps illustrate the often-arbitrary nature of national income accounting. One fundamental macroeconomic measurement is the gross domestic product (GDP) – an estimate of the total value of goods and services produced within an economy over a specific time period. Part of the process of developing the definition of GDP involves deciding what would and would not be included, and how money values could be assigned. One of the challenges the men who first designed the system of national accounts faced was deciding how the value of housing should be included in GDP. Renters were easy – you could just add up the amount paid in rent. But many people owned their homes and did not pay rents. How do you assign a value to housing services from owner-occupied houses and apartments?

The creators of the system of national accounts thought that only counting rents, and ignoring owner-occupied homes, would lead to a biased estimate of the contribution of housing to national income (Bos

---

2. The people closely associated with the creation and analysis of a system of national accounts were all men – to give a number of prominent examples: Simon Kuznets, Colin Clark, Wassily Leontief and Jan Tinbergen.

1992). One way of getting around this problem is to assign a value to the housing services of owner-occupied residences equal to what the owners would have to pay to rent an equivalent dwelling. Imputed rents became the basis for assigning a money value to housing services in GDP calculations. This is not a trivial amount. To give a concrete example, in 2016 estimates of the value of housing services for the US economy totaled $2 trillion of which approximately $1.5 trillion was the imputed rental value of owner-occupied housing.[3]

So what is the big deal? Using imputed rents to value housing services sounds like a reasonable solution to a challenging question. But here's where the problem lies – similar values could be imputed for other services, such as those produced using unpaid labour. The fact that values are assigned to owner-occupied homes, but not to non-market services is completely arbitrary. A house is an impassive structure, yet it is seen as generating services that are counted in a country's national income. Many of the services that are produced inside that house, the things that make a house a home, are not included – cleaning, cooking, and caring for others, to mention a few.

Non-market household production is just one segment of the broader economy that is excluded from standard macroeconomic measurements (CMEPSP 2010). For instance, chemical manufacturing may produce useful consumer goods, but also adds to the pollution of the environment. The value of the goods produced will raise GDP, but the costs of pollution are ignored. Quality of life may be poorly captured. If large numbers of people suffer from poor health, their medical treatment contributes to GDP. But maintaining good health is not reflected in typical macro indicators.

The following section of the book takes these issues of macroeconomic measurement seriously – with a focus on non-market production. The central argument is simple: taking into account non-market production is not only important for recognizing women's (and men's)

---

3. These figures come from the national income and product account database maintained by the Bureau of Economic Analysis, Department of Commerce, US Federal Government.

unpaid work and, ideally, would help reduce gender inequalities. If done carefully, it can also fundamentally change how we think about macroeconomics. To see why this is the case, we need to go back to basics and begin with the accounting relationships that underpin some of the foundational relationships of macroeconomic analysis.

RETHINKING MACROECONOMIC ACCOUNTING

A country's gross domestic product (GDP) represents one of the most important of the standard macroeconomic indicators. It is used to measure economic growth, to calculate average standards of living, and to draw conclusions about a population's well-being. GDP is a measure of the total market value, based on monetary prices often determined in the process of exchange, of goods and services newly produced within a country's borders over a given time period. Unpacking this definition, we see that GDP excludes certain economic transactions. For instance, only newly produced goods and services are counted. If you build a new house, the construction of the house is added to GDP. But if you sell an existing house you bought ten years ago for five times what you paid for it, the exchange is not included in the calculation of GDP, even though the sale generates income for the seller.

There are other economic activities that are also excluded from GDP. The most important of these for the current discussion are non-market household services produced with unpaid labour. The computation of GDP is based on the market value of goods and services produced within the economy. Goods and services that are not exchanged and do not have a clear market price may be excluded. In the system of national accounts, goods produced with unpaid labour for use within the household (i.e. not exchanged) are, at least theoretically, included in the calculation of GDP. However, arbitrarily, services produced with unpaid labour, such as non-market childcare, are excluded. Much of the unpaid work women do involves the production of non-market services.

The exclusion of non-market services from the most important indicator of overall macroeconomic activity does not make much sense. A meal prepared in a restaurant is counted, but a meal made at home is not. Paying someone to watch your children adds to GDP, but taking care of them yourself does not. The services provided by nursing homes boost GDP, but the value of similar services are ignored if people care for elderly relatives themselves. There are gender biases built into the way macroeconomic indicators are crafted. Since women typically do the bulk of this work, their economic contributions are erased.

A more complete reckoning of economic activity would include non-market services produced with unpaid labour. To see how the inclusion of non-market production would change macroeconomics, it is good to begin with the basic accounting expressions used to calculate GDP. To keep things simple, we will assume a closed economy, with no trade in goods and services and no globalization of production (e.g. a situation in which a company in one country owns factories overseas that generate profits for the head corporation). The expressions that follow can be modified fairly easily to capture cross-border production and exchange.

The expenditure approach

The most common way of computing GDP is to sum up the market value of expenditures on the production of final goods and services. Domestic expenditures are separated into three categories: private consumption expenditures, private investment expenditures, and government expenditures on goods and services.[4] The iconic macroeconomic equation, found in most introductory textbooks, that captures this approach to measuring GDP is:

(1) $GDP = Y = C + I + G$

---

4. Government expenditures that are money payments to households and businesses, but do not involve purchases of goods and services, are called transfer payments and are not included in the calculation of GDP.

Here the variable Y is used to represent GDP as a measure of the total income produced in an economy, C represents household consumption, I business investment, and G all government spending. The above equation expresses the idea that, at the macroeconomic level, the total market income generated in an economy is equal to the total amount spent on goods and services, and this also equals the total value of market production.

This version of the expenditure approach only focuses on market exchanges and government spending. To make this clear, we add a subscript "M" to signal market values.

(2) $GDP = Y_M = C_M + I_M + G$

Private expenditures are broken down into consumption and investment. But government spending is lumped together. Governments invest as well as consume. Think about government buildings, bridges, water and sewer systems, and roads. Furthermore, macroeconomic definitions of investment typically only count additions to the capital stock as investment, physical assets such as equipment and infrastructure that are used in production. But other types of public spending on less tangible productive capacities should also be consider investments. For instance, public education is usually treated as a type of consumption, even though a strong case could be made that educational expenditures raise productivity and contribute to growth. They have more in common with investments than they do with consumer goods, such as food or clothing. Separating government spending into public consumption and an expanded concept of public investment gives us a more nuanced representation of GDP.

(3) $GDP = Y_M = C_M + I_M + G_C + G_I$

For the purposes of this analysis, we define human capacities along the same lines as Braunstein, van Staveren and Tavani (2011). These refer to individual attributes that improve that person's productive contributions, both in terms of paid and unpaid labour. Human capacities are not innate, but must be built in the course of a person's life. They include formal education and training, i.e. the traditional categories of human capital, but also emotional maturity, leadership, the ability to work collaboratively, cultivated creativity, good health, and other similar attributes.

Governments are not the only ones that invest in building the capacities of human beings. Private expenditures also go towards maintaining and enhancing human resources, through education, health, and similar services. Moreover, in the standard GDP equation, private consumption is defined as being equivalent to all household expenditures on goods and services. But we have argued that households do not just consume, they also produce. Some goods that a household buys are used when producing household services. A washing machine is actually a capital investment used to produce laundry services at home. If we recognize that a lot of production takes place in the household, many types of consumer durables should be classified as investment rather than consumption. Taking these points into account, we can modify the GDP expression further.

(4) $\text{GDP} = Y_M = (C_M - I_{CD}) + I_M + I_{CD} + G_C + G_I$

What does this mean? $(C_M - I_{CD})$ represents total household spending less purchases of consumer durables that are, in reality, investments in household production. It indicates the amount that households spend on direct consumption. I_M and G_I represent private and public investment expenditures, respectively, but are now interpreted to include investments in human capacities (i.e. expenditures on people that yield some kind of future returns).

We have arrived at a modified definition of the components of GDP. But GDP still excludes non-market production, particularly of household and community services produced with unpaid labour. Non-market production contributes to direct consumption (e.g. eating a home cooked meal) and human investments (e.g. face-to-face interactions with small children that expand cognitive capacities). Therefore, non-market production can also be categorized as consumption or investment. Although non-market services do not represent household purchases, they can substitute for market expenditures and in a very real sense supplement market-based consumption and investment.

(5) $\text{NMP} = C_{NM} + I_{NM}$

Now we use the subscript "NM" to indicate non-market forms of production. If we add in non-market production, we are changing the definition of GDP and need to come up with a new term. For the purposes of this discussion, we will call the combination of market and non-market production of goods and services the expanded domestic product, or EDP.

(6) $\text{EDP} = \text{GDP} + \text{NMP} = (C_M - I_{CD} + C_{NM} + G_c) + (I_M + G_I + I_{CD} + I_{NM})$

The first term in parentheses represents total consumption in the economy – the sum of household market expenditures on consumption (net of consumer durables), government consumption, and non-market contributions to household consumption. Investment includes private market expenditures on investments, public investments, spending on consumer durables, and non-market investments in human beings.

The production approach

Adding up all expenditures on final goods and services is only one approach to calculating GDP. A second accounting technique that should yield the same result involves summing up the value of all goods and services produced in the economy. Although this sounds straightforward, and closely follows the formal definition of GDP, there are a few complications. Totalling the value of all output produced in the economy will significantly overstate the actual value of what is produced. Think of building a wooden table using inputs sourced domestically. The table requires wood, nails, varnish and other inputs. If we start with the value of the table, measured as its market price, and then add in the price of the wood used to produce the table, we end up double-counting the value of the wood. This is because the final price of the table already includes the value of the wood used to produce it.

Therefore, to calculate GDP by summing up the value of output produced, we need to subtract the value of intermediate inputs used in production. Another way of thinking about this approach is that GDP represents the total of the value-added produced in an economy, the additional value above the value of inputs used in production.

(7) GDP = market value of output − market value of intermediate inputs

How do we apply the production approach to non-market production (NMP)? The answer is simple: use the same method. The value-added of NMP would be the imputed value of non-market output less the market value of any intermediate inputs used. Suppose we wanted to value a dinner of pasta and a salad cooked and consumed at home using unpaid labour. Using the production approach, we would estimate the market value of the meal (e.g. what would we have to pay to purchase an equivalent prepared meal). However, not all the components of the meal are produced at home. Suppose we bought the pasta, a sauce and salad ingredients at a local supermarket. To avoid double-counting when producing an estimate of NMP, we would have to subtract the value of these market purchases from the imputed market value of the prepared meal.

(8) NMP = imputed value of non-market output − market value of intermediate inputs

If we subtract the market value of intermediate inputs from the imputed value of non-market output, what is left? Most of the difference in the value of a prepared meal and the value of all the purchased ingredients that go into the meal is simply the value of the unpaid labour used to produce the meal. This suggests that, following the production approach, the value-added of non-market production should be equal to the value of the unpaid labour used to produce it.

However, there are two additional sources of value that needs to be taken into account. Consumer durables are often used in non-market household production and they do not last forever. Over time, they wear out or depreciate. The value of this depreciation, over the productive life of consumer durables, should also be counted as part of non-market production.[5] If we represent the depreciation of consumer durables by D_{CD}, non-market production can be valued as follows:

(9)   NMP = imputed value of non-market output − market value of intermediate inputs = imputed value of unpaid labour + D_{CD}

Combining the expression for GDP and the expression for NMP yields a second way of arriving at an estimate of what we are calling the expanded domestic product or EDP.

(10)   EDP = market value of output + imputed value of non-market output − market value of intermediate inputs used in the production of market and non-market output ... or ...

(10a)   EDP = GDP + imputed value of unpaid labour + D_{CD}

In other words, we can arrive at an estimate of EDP by adding an imputed value of unpaid labour and an allowance for the depreciation of consumer durables to estimates of GDP, traditionally defined.

The income approach

There is a third way of coming up with a value for GDP − the income approach. When households, businesses, and governments spend

---

5. Intangible investments in human capacities also are subject to depreciation and a portion of this depreciation could be included in the calculation of what we are calling non-market production using the production approach. This type of depreciation is discussed later in the chapter.

money on goods and services, someone gets paid. These expenditures on production generate income that gets distributed in different ways, for example, as wages or profits. Therefore, the total value of production bought and sold should equal total expenditures which, in turn, should equal the total market income generated.

There is one complicating issue – depreciation. Suppose a company buys a piece of equipment that lasts for ten years. The initial purchase of the equipment counts as an investment expenditure and appears in GDP. However, each year that piece of equipment wears out little by little. The "using up" of the equipment represents an input into production that gets incorporated into the value of the final product produced. However, unlike purchases of raw materials, the depreciation of fixed assets, such as equipment and buildings, does not generate a stream of income beyond the initial investment. Only when the time comes to replace a worn-out piece of capital are new expenditures undertaken.

Therefore, the total income generated in an economy should equal the GDP less the estimated depreciation (D) of the private and public capital used in the production of goods and services. In a closed economy, without transfers of income to and from other countries, the difference between GDP and depreciation is referred to as national income.

(11) GDP – D = national income = wages/salaries + profits + rents + interest

National income is distributed in various ways. Wages and salaries are paid to employees that supply labour used in the production of goods and services. Profits represent the earnings of businesses, such as corporations and proprietorships, when they sell goods and services. Rents are payments made for the use of existing resources, such as the rent paid by the owner of a retail business to use space in a building. And interest payments represent income earned when households, governments, and companies lend money to each other.[6]

---

6. For this discussion, the various types of income, wages or profits, are before-tax income.

If we added up all these sources of income – wages, profits, rents and interest – and then adjust for depreciation, we should end up with the same measure of GDP, allowing for a few statistical discrepancies, that we would get if we applied the expenditure or production approach.

But families rely on more than the income earned through market exchanges. Non-market production underpins the ability of households to transform market transactions, such as buying groceries, into the things that they can actually use, such as a prepared meal. The purchase of goods and services, take-away meals or paid childcare, substitute, perhaps imperfectly, for non-market production at home. This means that household production, by generating real value added, raises living standards, and should be counted in indicators of macroeconomic activity and material well-being.

Non-market income (NMI) can be calculated using the same technique used to arrive at national income. Non-market income equals the imputed value of non-market production less depreciation. But why, in this case, does depreciation enter the picture? Recall that consumer durables represent a category of investment in assets that are used in non-market household production. Consumer durables do not last forever, and their depreciation is a real cost to households. Therefore, it makes sense to adjust non-market production by the amount of depreciation of consumer durables (D_{CD}) to yield non-market income, just as national income equals GDP less depreciation of fixed assets.

(12) $NMI = NMP - D_{CD}$ = imputed value of unpaid labour

Notice that when we subtract the depreciation of consumer durables from non-market production, we are simply left with the imputed value of unpaid labour.

The last step would be to combine market income and non-market income to get a measure of expanded national income. But there is a final consideration. Durable goods, whether they are fixed capital equipment or consumer durables, are not the only productive resources that depreciate. Investments in human capacities are also subject to depreciation. For the purposes of macroeconomic accounting, what we are concerned with here is any depreciation of human investments that occurs in the process of market and non-market production. People occasionally become injured or fall ill when engaged in productive activities. This represents a form of depreciation. New investments, for example, medical services, are needed to restore a person's productive capacities. Just as pieces of equipment can become obsolete, so can skills and, over time, aspects of the human capital people have acquired in the course of their lives need updating. Again, investment is needed to restore people's productive capacities. Therefore, we must adjust expanded national income to take into account the depreciation of human investments, D_{HI}.

The expression for expanded national income therefore becomes:

(13) $\quad \text{ENI} = \text{EDP} - D - D_{CD} - D_{HI} = \text{wages} + \text{profits} + \text{rents} + \text{interest} + \text{NMI}$

The three different ways of incorporating non-market production into the standard methods for computing GDP – the expenditure approach, the production approach, and the income approach – give us different, yet related, macroeconomic interpretations of non-market production and unpaid work. The expenditure approach highlights how non-market production contributes to consumption and investment. The production approach demonstrates that the value-added of non-market production should be equal to the imputed value of the unpaid labour used plus an allowance for the depreciation of consumer durables. The income approach illustrates how unpaid work raises living standards in ways ignored in traditional macroeconomic measurements. However, the implications of these adjustments go beyond a question of measurement. They also alter the ways key macroeconomic relationships are interpreted.

USE OF INCOME AND THE SAVINGS/INVESTMENT IDENTITY

The income generated in the economy is put to various uses. Some is spent on consumption (C), some is saved (S), and some is transferred to the government in the form of taxes (T). Turning back to the expenditure approach and putting aside the question of government consumption for a moment, we see that total private consumption is equal to $C_M - I_{CD} + C_{NM}$ (Equation 6). That is, private consumption equals market consumption net of consumer durables plus that part of non-market production that supplements household consumption. Private savings also comes from the market economy and is equal to the portion of household income not spent on consumption and profits that are reinvested in a business. But there is also a non-market component of savings. After all, savings is simply the portion of income not consumed. So the portion of non-market income that does not supplement direct consumption, i.e. the portion of non-market production that represents investments in human beings, is equal to non-market savings.

This suggests that expanded national income, what we are calling ENI, should equal total consumption (market and non-market), total savings (market and non-market), and taxes transferred to the government.

$$(14) \quad ENI = EDP - D - D_{CD} - D_{HI} = C_M - I_{CD} + C_{NM} + S_M + S_{NM} + T$$

Substituting the expression for EDP from the expenditure approach (Equation 6) gives us:

$$(15) \quad (C_M - I_{CD} + C_{NM} + G_c) + (I_M + G_I + I_{CD} + I_{NM}) - D - D_{CD} - D_{HI} = C_M - I_{CD} + C_{NM} + S_M + S_{NM} + T$$

A number of terms appear on both sides of Equation 15. The expression can be simplified.

$$(16) \quad (I_M + G_I + I_{NM} - D - D_{HI}) + (I_{CD} - D_{CD}) = S_M + S_{NM} + (T - G_c)$$

What does Equation 16 signify? The expression $(I_M + G_I + I_{NM} - D - D_{HI})$ is simply private market investment, public investment, and non-market investment less the value of the capital and human investments that have depreciated. This is an expression for what we call net investment, i.e. the amount of investment above that needed to replace capital that has worn out and the human investments that have depreciated. Along the same lines, the expression $(I_{CD} - D_{CD})$ is simply net investment in consumer durables. The entire left side of Equation 16 represents total net investment in the economy. In contrast, the right-hand side indicates the total amount of savings: market savings, non-market savings and government savings. Government savings is just the amount of government revenue (T) that is not spent on consumption (G_C).

Put another way, Equation 16 represents the familiar macroeconomic identity that equates aggregate investment with aggregate savings. So, what is new? Unlike the traditional approaches to the investment/savings relationship, this expression redefines what is meant by investment and includes non-market production. This changes how we analyze and understand macroeconomics. To see this, we can return to the more traditional approach by excluding non-market production, treating all government expenditure the same, and including spending on consumer durables as part of consumption, not investment. Making these adjustments turns Equation 16 into a textbook expression of the investment/savings relationship.

$$(17) \quad (I_M - D) = S_M + (T - G)$$

Although seemingly innocuous, this expression lies at the epicentre of some hotly contested macroeconomic debates. It states that net private investment equals private savings plus government savings, the difference between taxes and spending. One interpretation of this identity argues that increases in government spending (G) will reduce the right-hand side of the identity and cause net private investment to fall. Government spending is said to "crowd out" private investment. But this is not the only way to interpret this relationship. An alternative story, often labelled "Keynesian", is that an autonomous increase in investment generates additional income in the economy, perhaps by raising overall levels of employment. Savings rise with income, until the investment-equals-savings relationship is restored. In this version, inadequate savings is a result of a failure to mobilize investment, not because of too much government spending.

The point here is not to resolve the investment/savings debate, but rather to demonstrate that the ways in which macroeconomic variables and relationships are defined have huge implications for understanding how economies work and the implications for policy. Seemingly simple changes such as incorporating non-market production into these models and redefining what counts as investment change macroeconomic thinking. To see this, we return to the expanded investment/savings relationship.

(18) $(I_M + G_I - D) + (I_{CD} - D_{CD}) + I_{NM} = S_M + S_{NM} + (T - G_C)$

One implication of this more comprehensive approach to investment and saving is that non-market household production can actually support private fixed capital investment in the market economy. Suppose that there is an increase in non-market production. This can have two effects. It may raise the amount of non-market savings that support investments in human beings through unpaid caring labour. In addition, it may raise the amount of non-market consumption. If non-market consumption substitutes for at least a portion of market consumption, a rise in non-market consumption may reduce expenditures on market consumption and raise household savings. This frees up resources that can be used for private fixed investment.

We can use this same expanded identity to look at a second example, one that explores the possible effects of a rise in women's labour force participation, i.e. participation in paid employment, on macroeconomic outcomes. A common argument is that increases in women's labour force participation will raise GDP and help support growth. However, what this argument fails to acknowledge is that this holds by definition. If women spend less time in non-market production, which is not counted as part of GDP, and spend more time in market production, which is counted, GDP will inevitably rise. But the picture based on a more comprehensive acounting is less clear. Does the increase in the value produced by paid labour fully offset the loss of non-market income?

One scenario is that the decline in non-market production reduces non-market savings, while the increase in market income raises overall consumption. The result would be lower net investment, specifically investments in human capacities, and less savings. Of course, higher market consumption may, in the medium term, encourage more investment in the market economy and help to offset the initial fall in non-market investment. Much depends on the use of the market income women earn when they enter the workforce or increase their hours of paid work. It may be used to purchase substitutes for non-market investments, such as paid childcare. It may be used to purchase consumer durables that increase the productivity of the unpaid labour used in non-market production.

These are just a few of the examples of how the expanded investment/savings relationship transforms how we think about macroeconomics. It also alters policy analysis. Government spending on education can "crowd-in" private investment by increasing the long-run productivity of the economy's human resources. This is easier to see if public spending on building human capacities is counted as an investment, which generates returns over time, rather than simply a consumption expenditure.

CALCULATING NON-MARKET PRODUCTION

Expanding the standard macroeconomic accounting framework to include non-market production and unpaid labour poses one critical challenge – how do we assign a value to this production if there are no market prices? The general idea of including goods and services that are not exchanged in the calculation of GDP and national income is not daunting. Indeed, it is routinely done. The public sector produces goods and services that have no clear market price based on exchange, and yet the activities of the various levels of government form an important part of the calculation of national income. Clearly, the market exchange of final goods and services is not a prerequisite for economic activities to be included in the national accounts.

There is one significant difference between government production and non-market household production. Public employees are paid a salary, but much of non-market household production remains unpaid.

The value of government production can therefore be based on the cost of the labour used in the public sector. There is no equivalent wage bill for non-market household production.

To help solve this problem, we turn to the three approaches for assigning a value to the productive activities that take place in an economy – the expenditure approach, the production approach, and the income approach. We can dispense with the income approach fairly quickly. Since non-market household production is unpaid, no direct payments are made to the productive factors used, such as labour or consumer durables. This is not to say that non-market production has no impact on living standards. It clearly does. But there are no observable monetary payments, making this a difficult accounting framework to apply.

It seems equally problematic to use the expenditure approach, since no expenditures are actually made – except in terms of market goods that are inputs into household production (e.g. groceries). However, we could argue that, if household production did not occur, households would have to buy equivalent services elsewhere. They would have to use paid childcare or purchase already-prepared meals. The prices of these substitutes could be used to assign a value to non-market household production. This is the approach used to value *goods* produced with non-market labour in the official GDP measures. If a family grew food in a small garden plot for their own use, that food would be valued at what it would have cost them to purchase the equivalent amount of food in the market. Recall that non-market *services* are excluded from official GDP calculations. But this does not prevent a similar valuation approach being applied to services produced at home.

One potential roadblock for using the expenditure approach is that it may be difficult to find good market substitutes for non-market household services. There can be differences in the meals one gets at restaurants or through delivery services and the kinds of meals prepared at home. Are babysitters or childcare centres able to provide the same quality of care as a parent? If ailing, elderly relatives would rather be cared for by family members, at home, instead of being placed in a nursing home, can we really say that the market and non-market services provided are equivalent? At a practical level, there may not be enough detailed data about the actual output, in terms of quality and quantity, of services produced at home to assign a clear value using the expenditure approach.

This brings us to the production approach. As we saw earlier, the production approach would set the value of non-market household production equal to the value of unpaid work used plus an allowance for the depreciation of consumer durables.[7] This has an intuitive appeal. The primary source of value-added of non-market services comes directly from the labour used in their production. Furthermore, it is the same approach currently used to value public sector goods and services. The productive contribution of government to GDP is typically measured as being equivalent to the inputs used to produce public services, the largest component of which are the wages and salaries paid to public sector workers (CMEPSP 2010).

To apply the production approach, we need information on how much time women and men spend producing non-market household services. Standard sources of data on paid employment are of little help. Much of the information on employment, unemployment, hours of work, and wages paid come from labour force surveys. However, the boundary for what is included and excluded from labour force surveys is typically the same as the boundary set for the national accounts. Since the production of non-market, household services is not recognized in GDP measurements, variables capturing the labour used to produce these services is absent from most labour force surveys.

Because of this, a different approach is needed. Data from time-use surveys, not labour force surveys, come to the rescue. Time-use surveys provide detailed information on how individuals use their time in the course of a day and can be used to estimate the quantity of, and assign a value to, unpaid household labour. Well-designed surveys break down the time spent with regard to specific activities, taking into account the fact that people may be performing multiple tasks simultaneously (e.g. making dinner and keeping an eye on the kids). This provides a picture

---

7. As discussed earlier, adjustments could also be made based on the depreciation of investment in human capacities.

of the total amount of time spent in different, non-market activities. A detailed discussion of the analysis of time-use data is beyond the scope of this book. But without careful analysis of quality time-use data, reliable estimates of the value of non-market household work would be difficult to generate.

Once the amount of unpaid labour is known, the next step is to value it. The most common way of assigning a monetary value to unpaid labour is to determine what that labour would have earned in the marketplace if it had been paid rather than unpaid. But which wage rate is the correct one? There are a large number of options, and the choice hinges on how we want to value household services. One approach would be to treat all unpaid work as relatively unskilled. For instance, the labour used to raise a child would be valued at a similar level as the wage one would pay a babysitter to watch the children. A baseline wage, such as the minimum wage, could be used, or the average prevailing wage of unskilled workers.

But not all unpaid labour is the same. Some unpaid labour involves routine activities. But other activities demand a significant amount of responsibility and decision-making. The intensity of work varies with the kinds of services being provided. The education and experience of the person supplying the unpaid labour affects the quality of the services delivered. Ideally, the value assigned to unpaid labour would take these issues into account.

Economists Jooyeoun Suh and Nancy Folbre developed an approach for estimating the value of unpaid childcare for the US economy that recognizes that many different types of labour go into raising a child (Suh & Folbre 2014). Their calculations are based on information generated by the American Time Use Survey, but they go beyond a simple calculation of time spend doing childcare valued at a single, basic wage rate. In their estimates, they adjust for the intensity of different care services and the number of children present. They use specialist wages, adjusted for the educational attainment of the care provider, to assign values to a range of unpaid childcare activities. For example, basic supervisory labour – that is, simply keeping an eye on the children, perhaps while doing other household tasks – is valued less than developmental labour – such as reading to children, helping with school work, or performing other at-home educational services. By explicitly recognizing differences in the types of labour supplied and the activities performed, they produce a more accurate valuation of unpaid childcare.

There is one additional, fairly minor point, about valuing non-market household production in a macroeconomic context that should be mentioned. Consider a for-profit childcare centre. If you were to purchase services from this centre, the price would primarily reflect the cost of the labour used to provide the care. However, since the company makes a profit from these services, the price would not be precisely equal to the cost; there would be an additional mark-up. The value-added of the for-profit childcare services would be distributed between the wages paid and the profits made.

Compare this to our discussion of the valuation of non-market services. Using the production approach, those services are only valued in terms of their labour input, plus an allowance for the depreciation of capital used in non-market production. This could mean that the equivalent services purchased in the market would be valued more highly than non-market services, simply because the former would include a share going to profits.[8] This discrepancy drives a wedge between non-market services valued in terms of the labour used and the same services valued in terms of the price of market substitutes. For the purposes of the current discussion, this is a fairly minor detail, but it does reflect an inconsistency with regard to market valuations compared to non-market valuations based on labour inputs alone.

Efforts to extend the standard national accounting framework have resulted in the creation of what are called "satellite accounts"

---

8. The share of value-added distributed in the form of profit is often considered a payment to the capital assets used in production. This raises a question of whether the use of capital assets should be valued in non-market household production. Accounting conventions treat many of the productive assets purchased by households as consumption expenditures, not investments. This gets back to the issue of treating consumer durables as a form of investment. If consumer durables are counted as a type of productive asset, then their contribution to household production (e.g. increased productivity) could be measured and valued.

– measurements of parts of the economy that are not included in the official GDP statistics (CMEPSP 2010). Satellite accounts have been produced in an attempt to quantify a range of economic contributions, including those of the environment, tourism and unpaid labour. Using these kinds of satellite accounts, the interactions between the various sectors of the economy – for example, firms, governments, households, and the environment – can be captured in a detailed set of accounting relationships called a "social accounting matrix". The production of satellite accounts and social accounting matrices represents an important step forward in macroeconomic measurement. They make visible what was previously hidden and ignored.

Yet satellite accounts remain distant from most macroeconomic analysis and policy-making, just as orbiting satellites are far removed from the day-to-day events on the surface of planet earth. What is needed, as the previous discussion of macroeconomic accounting relationships demonstrated, is to bring non-market production and unpaid labour into the framework used to understand how the economy actually works. Doing so will change how we think about macroeconomics.

TRANSFER PAYMENTS, MACROECONOMICS AND LIVING STANDARDS

In the system of national accounts, some payments reflect market exchanges, such as when consumers purchase goods from firms, when businesses invest in new equipment, or when employees get paid for their labour. But there are other payments that are made without a direct exchange of goods or services. Think of the taxes paid to government. Households may also get income support from the state, and government may subsidize small businesses or large corporations. Payments that are made without a direct exchange of goods and services are called transfer payments.

When we think of the simple system of national accounts, putting aside international transactions, there are three main categories of economic actors – households, firms and governments. The accounting relationships take into account transfers between these categories, the most common of those being net transfers (taxes minus subsidies) from households and firms to the government. Payments between households and firms featured in the national accounts tend to involve market exchanges and not transfers. Households purchase goods and services from firms and supply labour. Firms purchase capital goods from other firms – which, within the standard approach to national accounts, we call investment.

However, transfers also occur between businesses and households. For example, if a household owns stock and receives a dividend payment, this represents a transfer from a corporation – a portion of the profits are transferred to households. Taking into account these transfers allows us to calculate the total income of households, often called personal income in the system of national accounts. Recall the expanded definition of national income that includes non-market production:

(19)   ENI = wages + profits + rents + interest + NMI

Households receive certain components of this expanded approach to calculating national income – specifically, wages and non-market income. But households also transfer income to governments and businesses, and, at the same time, they receive transfers from the public and private sectors. Households pay taxes and some families get income support or are provided services through government programmes. Wealthier households own financial assets and receive payments from businesses.

Adjusting household income to reflect these transfers gives us an expression for calculating personal income.

(20)   Personal Income = wages + NMI + receipts on assets (transfers from business) + net transfers from government

In this expanded definition, non-market production increases the size of household income compared to traditional calculations of personal income that ignore unpaid work.

A bit more needs to be said about government transfers and personal income. When it comes to government transfers, standard approaches to national income accounting only consider money transfers to and from households, such as taxes paid and income grants to low-income families. But households receive services directly from the government that do not involve money transfers. This kind of direct service provision is typically excluded from calculations of personal or household income. Excluding these services results in another macro mis-measurement. In the same way that non-market household production raises living standards, government services have a similar impact on household well-being.

Think about the following illustrative example. Suppose that there were two models to get medical care to people: (1) healthcare could be purchased entirely from private providers through market exchanges, or (2) the government could pay providers for their services and finance a national health programme through taxes. Assume further that the costs of option 1 and option 2 are identical and people get the same quality of care in both cases. If healthcare were provided under option 1, there would be no impact on the measurement of personal income of households. The spending on healthcare would simply reflect one use of personal income. However, if healthcare were provided under option 2, measured personal income would be lower, since the payment in the form of taxes would be subtracted from household income as a transfer to the government. This seems counter-intuitive, since households would be paying the identical amount for the same quality of care in both cases.

The problem could be solved if, under option 2, the value of the healthcare services received were counted as a transfer from the government, even if there is no monetary payment involved. By failing to count the value of direct service provision by the government, the usual approaches for computing personal income are biased. Once again, the non-market provision of services is discounted in the standard macro-economic framework. In this case, non-market service provision comes from the government, but the issue is remarkably similar to the exclusion of non-market service provision that comes from unpaid household

51

labour. For these reasons, "net transfers from government" should include the value of direct service provision to households.

The expression for calculating personal income in Equation 20 recognizes transfers between households and the government and business sectors of the economy. However, not all transfers occur across these general categories. A significant amount of transfers occurs *within* these categories. Most significant are transfers from one household to another. Working-age adults may support aging relatives. Young adults, fresh out of universities, may get money from their parents to help them make the transition from school to work. Marriages are occasions often marked by inter-household transfers. There are, of course, the wedding presents given to the married couple. In some cultures, a dowry is paid (a transfer from the bride's family to the groom's). In other societies, the groom must pay a bride-price (a transfer to the bride's family for the loss of a daughter). When marriages dissolve, one partner may pay alimony or child support to the other partner – another type of inter-household transfer.

If we extend our thinking to include non-market services and unpaid labour, transfers of time, not only money, take place between households. When a neighbour offers to watch the next-door children when their parents are away, the neighbour is, in effect, transferring time from one household to another. This time represents real economic resources. Without the help, the parents would have had to hire someone to take care of the children and the neighbour could have put this labour toward some other use. These transfers, as important as they are, disappear from macroeconomic measurement.

The reason for the vanishing transfers is fairly simple. Households both receive and make transfers. If we want to know whether households experience an inflow or outflow of resources, we want to look at net transfers – that is, transfers received from other households less transfers made to other households. However, at the macroeconomic level, net transfers, summed across all households, must be equal to zero. The total amount that households receive, in time and money, from other households must be equal to the total amount of transfers all households, taken together, make to others.

This raises a challenge to macroeconomic accounting. Simply because aggregate inter-household transfers must equal zero, putting aside the question of income transfers across borders, does not mean that such transfers will have no macroeconomic consequences. A family that receives help from relatives by taking care of children may be able to save more and invest more in their children's future compared to families receiving no help. This increase in savings and investment could be greater than any reduction in savings on the part of the relatives who volunteered to spend time with the kids. The net effect would be a positive increase in investments in human capacities. In other words, transfers of time and money between households (as well as between governments and households) can have broad-based impacts, even when these transfers disappear at the aggregate level. We will return to the macroeconomic implications of transfer payments, including inter-household transfers, in Chapter 3.

The existence of transfers of time and money between households also has implications for how we measure standards of living. The expanded definition of personal income gives us a new measurement of household income that includes non-market production. Dividing this aggregate income by the population yields an estimate of per capita income that includes market and non-market components. But this measurement obscures heterogeneity between households. Economies exhibit a great deal of wage inequality and therefore income from paid work will vary across households. Households differ in terms of the amount of unpaid work they perform and, as a result, so does the amount of non-market income they generate. Taxes paid and transfers from the government typically help reduce some of the inequalities in money income. But households also hold varying amounts of wealth and carry different debt burdens. Unlike government transfers, transfers to and from the private business sector may exacerbate inequalities rather than narrow them.

If transfers between households, businesses, and governments have a substantial impact on living standards, we should certainly take into account inter-household transfers of time and money. Consider two single-mother households, each with a two-year old child and identical incomes from employment. The mothers pay the same amount in taxes and qualify for the same income-support programmes from the government. However, one of the single mothers is able to drop her child off at her parents who take care of their grandchild, spending time and money, while the mother is at work. The second single mother has no relatives and must make arrangements for childcare – which often cost a significant amount. Who has the higher standard of living? Clearly, the first mother is better off, but we would not know this from standard measurements of income and poverty, which do not take into account either unpaid labour or inter-household transfers.

What this all means is that transfer payments, specifically inter-household transfers matter for understanding macroeconomic dynamics and relationships. They also matter for an accurate assessment of living standards and inequalities between households. Transfers often represent a reallocation of resources across generations: working adults helping out aging parents or taxes used to support programmes that invest in children. These intergenerational transfers are indispensible to maintaining our societies over time.

FROM SHORT TO LONG RUN

We have argued that the macroeconomic concepts and measurements at the core of policy-making and analysis are flawed. Numerous flaws exist, but the particular shortcoming emphasized in this book is the failure to include non-market household production. It is a gender issue because a disproportionate share of the unpaid labour used to produce household services is done by women. Women's economic contributions, critical as they are, are erased if they involve household labour or take place outside of the market. As a result, standard measurements of economic performance, growth, living standards, and well-being are inaccurate. This can lead to erroneous conclusions. Government spending does not always "crowd-out" investments, particularly when investments in human beings are acknowledged. Increasing women's participation in paid employment is not inevitably good for macroeconomic performance. Ambiguities exist.

The extended accounting framework proposed in this Chapter adopts a relatively short-run perspective. It takes a snap-shot of economic relationships over a relatively short period of time. The various macroeconomic adjustments that insure that savings equals investment, adopting the broader definitions of these terms, also take place in the short run.

But the macroeconomic implications are more far-reaching. It takes time, as well as a lot of resources, to raise the next generation. Unpaid labour not only supplies services, it produces the people that, in time, will make contributions that allow the economy to continue to operate. Some of the most important aspects of non-market household production involve long-run investments that yield future returns. But there are no guarantees. Decisions taken by individuals and households may not be the ones that support long-run economic performance. In some cases, fertility rates may be too high relative to the number of job opportunities available when the children grow up. In other cases, too few children and an aging population have serious implications for an economy's long-run trajectory.

The next chapter takes on this challenge and looks at the long-run implications of the gender and household dynamics that, although frequently ignored, shape the future of our economies.

3

Reimagining macro: gender and economics in the long run

Most macroeconomists identify economic progress with growth – a sustained increase in GDP, or GDP per capita, over time. But relying on GDP has its shortcomings. Standard national income statistics fail to capture many features of the economy that are important to our well-being. Plus, these measurements are not the best indicator of household living standards, since they ignore non-market production, do not fully reflect transfers, and fail to accurately capture the benefits of direct government services. Nevertheless, increases in national income are imperfectly correlated, at least on average, with outcomes people care about, such as living longer and healthier lives, enjoying better living conditions, and having more choices in the course of their lives. When growth turns negative, as happens during recessions and depressions, the effect can be devastating. People lose their livelihoods and feel their economic security evaporate. For these reasons, understanding the factors that contribute to long-run economic performance at the macro level remains an area of concern.

Robert Solow, a prolific US economist, is intimately associated with one early, and extremely influential, approach to theorizing growth at the macro level. The original Solow growth model identifies two factors of production that determine total market output: capital and labour (Solow 1956). In the Solow model, capital refers to investment in productive, physical assets, such as equipment, buildings and machinery. Labour represents the total volume of paid work that employed people perform. In most versions of the original Solow model, there is a technology parameter that increases the productivity of capital, or labour, or both factors simultaneously. In the model, capital is a produced factor of production, meaning that a certain fraction of total output is reserved for building more machines, equipment, production facilities, and other forms of physical investment. In contrast, factors outside of the macroeconomy determine the amount of labour available. In the basic model, population growth rates are fixed and are not influenced by the process of production or the accumulation of capital assets over time.

When it comes to modeling economic growth, capital has always had the pride of place as the quintessential produced factor of production. The Solow growth model is not alone in this regard. Other early theories of economic growth also focus on how capital is produced and accumulated (see, e.g., Kaldor 1957; Harrod 1939). There have been numerous elaborations on the basic Solow model over time. In one variation, technology is produced along with capital – part of the economy produces goods and services while another part engages in knowledge production, pushing out the technology frontier (Romer 1990). In another version of the Solow model, both physical capital and human capital, in this case formal education and training, are produced and contribute to the GDP (Barro 2001; Mankiw, Romer & Weil 1992).

It is much less common for macroeconomists to recognize that the people who inhabit an economy are also produced. Just as a fraction of output is reserved for investment in physical capital, investing in children requires goods and services, such as food, clothing, healthcare and education. Turning children into productive adults also takes a good deal of time and requires a combination of market and non-market production. Yet most macroeconomic models, including the original Solow model, assume that labour is produced outside of, and is unaffected by, the macroeconomy. There are exceptions to this: growth models in which economic dynamics affect population growth (Barro & Becker 1989; Galor & Weil 1996; Jones 1997; Doepke & Tertilt 2016; Agénor 2017). Still, the realm of macroeconomics is generally content to ignore the fact that the human resources that run the economy are themselves produced.

The irony is that without population growth, the economy will eventually grind to a halt. Set the population growth rate to zero in these models and economic growth eventually disappears. In the short run, GDP growth may continue in the absence of population growth if there are technological improvements that raise the productivity of the existing labour force. This could last for several years, or possibly even decades. But without a next generation to take over, the economy is no longer sustainable. Despite all of the advances in automation and artificial intelligence, we have not yet advanced to a stage where economies can dispense of human beings altogether.

Most macroeconomic theories fail to deal with the question of how societies reproduce themselves. In most approaches, it happens automatically. A better macroeconomics would take this issue much more seriously and treat human beings as one of the products of the economies in which they live. Producing the next generation is a gendered process. Women perform a disproportionate share of the unpaid work that goes into reproducing our societies. Women also tend to be segregated into types of paid employment that involve the care of other people, such as teachers and nurses. Health and education services represent examples of investments in human beings that yield future returns and underpin economic performance. Women's work, both paid and unpaid, is essential for the long-run health of an economy, yet these contributions are poorly integrated into macroeconomic thinking. This chapter takes a close look at human investment, gender inequality and long-run economic performance.

DEMOGRAPHICS AND MACROECONOMICS

The idea that population dynamics affect economic performance is not new. One of the best-known theories of how populations and economics interact was developed at the turn of the eighteenth century by Thomas Malthus, well before the term "macroeconomics" was first used. Malthus was a British clergyman and scholar whose gloomy pronouncements on the relationship between population growth and material well-being earned economics the moniker "the dismal science".

In *An Essay on the Principle of Population*, Malthus argued that improvements in average incomes, thanks to economic growth, would have grave consequences (Malthus 2004). He thought that higher living standards would cause families to have more children. The population would initially expand along with national income. But this growing population would eventually trigger an economic backlash. This is because population growth occurred without a similar increase in the other resources, such as land, required to produce the things people needed to survive. Over time, productivity would fall as a growing population crowded a relatively finite stock of economic resources, driving average living standards down. As incomes fell below the subsistence level, more people would begin to die. Mortality rates would rise to counteract the higher birth rates. In effect, poverty and death became the punishment for having too many children and would discipline population dynamics in the face of economic growth.

The dire predictions of Thomas Malthus never came to pass. There are a number of reasons why. Malthus was primarily writing about a pre-industrial society in which it could be reasonable to think that economic resources were finite. At the time he was writing, land and natural resources were the primary factors of production and assumed to be relatively fixed. With industrialization and the expansion of capitalism, this was no longer the case. Physical capital could be produced and the stock of capital expanded over time. Furthermore, technological improvements caused productivity to increase, rather than population growth causing productivity to fall. Importantly, higher incomes did not unequivocally lead to booming fertility rates. Indeed, fertility rates tend to be lower for countries with higher per capita income. Malthus did not get the economics of population dynamics right.

Although his gloom and doom theory of population was off the mark, in some ways Malthus was visionary. He was the first to propose a connection between demographic change and, what we call today, macroeconomics. As the discipline of macroeconomics developed in the twentieth century, these demographic concerns were expunged from most theories of growth. But there are important reasons for reconsidering the relationship between population dynamics and long-run growth. Here we discuss two real-world examples: youth bulges and below-replacement fertility.

Countries, particularly lower-income countries in sub-Saharan Africa and South Asia, have large youth populations relative to the working-age population. High fertility rates contribute to the persistence of a relatively youthful population. If we consider the world average, in 2016, the number of people 15 years old or less was about 40 per cent of the number of working-age people, defined here as those between the ages of 15 and 64. Globally, the average fertility rate was 2.3 births for each woman. However, in sub-Saharan Africa, the number of people aged 15 years or less was 79 per cent of the number of people aged 15 to 64 in the same year. The fertility rate in sub-Saharan Africa was also higher – 4.8 births per woman on average.[1]

What does this mean? For countries with large youth populations, there are fewer working-age adults per child or young person to generate income and perform unpaid care work. This means that we would expect the amount of time and economic resources invested in each child to be lower. If fewer investments are made in the next generation, this would affect the productive capacities of the future labour force as young people grow up and become working adults. Insufficient human investments affect the productivity of the economy as a whole.

A large youth population could be an advantage, since all those human resources could unleash a huge amount of productive potential. Some people call this the "demographic dividend", the boost to development that can be achieved when a large youth population enters its prime working ages. However, getting the benefits of a demographic dividend is tough. There must be sufficient job opportunities available to these young workers for their productive potential to be realized. If they end up unemployed, their economic potential is squandered. Studies also suggest that, for a demographic dividend to be realized, fertility rates must fall, so that the size of the youth population comes into balance with other age groups over time (Bloom, Canning & Sevilla 2002).

---

1. These statistics come from the World Development Indicators database, World Bank, Washington, DC.

An illustration helps show the connections between demographics and macroeconomics. Figure 3.1 below shows the age distributions of two countries, the Republic of Korea and Kenya, back in 1960. At that time, both countries had large youth populations relative to the size of the working-age population. They were also both poor countries. Kenya's average annual income was around $540 (measured in US dollars at their 2010 level) while income per person in South Korea was better, around $945, but less than twice as high. Fast forward to 2017. The new age distributions of the population are shown in Figure 3.2. The general shape of the distribution in Kenya is similar to what it was over five decades earlier. However, for Korea the relative size of the youth population has fallen noticeably, while the size of the working-age population has grown (An & Jeon 2006). In 2017, the average GDP per capita in Kenya had more than doubled, to $1,170 – again valued in US dollars at their 2010 level. Over 50 years later, Kenya had surpassed Korea's income in 1960. But in the meantime, Korea's per capita income had soared to over $26,000 – 27 times what it was back in 1960.[2]

The comparison of Korea and Kenya shows that there is a connection between the demographic structure of a country and its economic development, although the direction of causation is not clear. One way of telling the Korean story is that the country's large youth population represented a pool of labour that fueled economic development (e.g. Bloom & Finlay 2009). At the same time, falling fertility rates reduced the relative size of the youth population over time, which facilitated more investment in each child. All of these changes gave the economy a productive boost. But the story could be told in the reverse direction: that economic development came first and caused the demographic change. In this version, economic development increased the costs of having children, as new opportunities became available to women and the amount spent on each child's education and personal development increased. As costs rose, fertility rates fell.

---

2. Statistics on per capita income come from the World Development Indicators database. World Bank, Washington, DC.

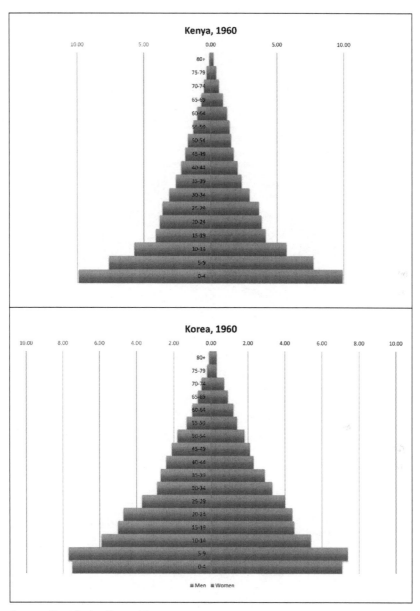

Source: PopulationPyramid.net

Figure 3.1 Percentage share of population by age group, Kenya and Korea, 1960

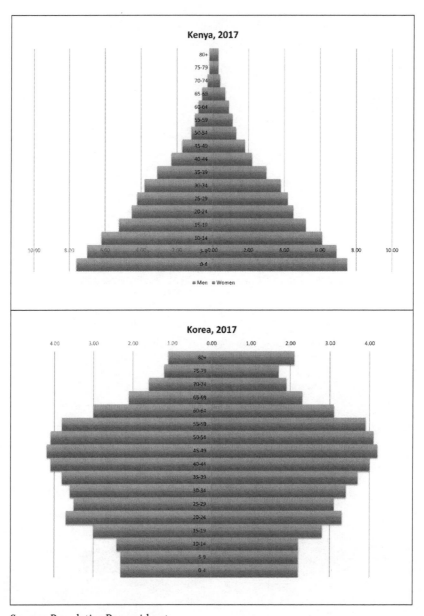

Source: PopulationPyramid.net

Figure 3.2 Percentage share of population by age group, Kenya and Korea, 2017

The true story is most likely a mixture of the two. Demographic changes affect economic development, and shifts in the structure of the economy affect families and fertility decisions. Although the gloomy predictions of Malthus never materialized, he did understand that macroeconomics and demographics were intimately linked in the long run. This lesson is routinely ignored in much of modern macroeconomic thinking.

Falling fertility rates might have served Korea well during the time it was industrializing, but low fertility is not necessarily a good thing. These days, Korea is more likely to be concerned that fertility is too low rather than too high. In high-income countries, where child mortality is quite low, average fertility rates need to be maintained at just about two children per woman to maintain the size of the population. Anything lower than that and the population will shrink over time. For developing countries, with higher rates of infant and child mortality, fertility rates must be higher to maintain population numbers.

Analysis from the United Nations found that, over the period 2010–15, 46 per cent of the world's population lived in countries with below replacement fertility.[3] In 2016, Korea's fertility rate was estimated to be 1.2 births per woman and Japan's was 1.5 births per women.[4] Most of Western Europe now has below-replacement fertility.[5] In the United States, in 2016, the average fertility rate was an estimated 1.8 births per woman. In all these cases, fertility rates have fallen below replacement levels.

What does this mean for the macroeconomy? It is hard to tell since the world of sustained below-replacement fertility remains largely unchartered territory. For countries with below-replacement fertility, the size of the youth population will shrink and the size of the older population, those over 65 years old, will grow. This raises serious questions about the changes needed to maintain pension and healthcare systems over time. Below-replacement fertility could also cause the size of the

---

3. United Nations, *World Population Prospects: 2017 Revision*.
4. World Development Indicators database.
5. United Nations, *World Population Prospects: 2017 Revision*.

future workforce to decline. A fall in the stock of one of the most important economic resources, human beings, will almost certainly have far-reaching consequences for the structure of the world's economies. Macroeconomic models and theories need to start taking these issues into account.

One strategy for maintaining a productive labour force when fertility rates have sunk below replacement levels is to get the people from somewhere else. The US currently has below-replacement fertility rates, but it also accepts a large number of immigrants each year who help maintain a growing population. Parents in other countries spent time and money raising these immigrants and turning them into productive adults. Countries like the US benefit from the human investments made elsewhere when immigrants make productive contributions to the US economy. It is similar to an inflow of foreign investment, but in the form of human beings and their capacities, rather than capital goods.

The important point is to recognize that demographics matter for macroeconomics and that gender dynamics represent an important force behind demographic trends. Yet most macroeconomic theory remains dismally underdeveloped when it comes to these issues. It is not only a question of getting the macroeconomics right. Gender inequalities underpin the way societies reproduce themselves. If these connections are ignored, we are unlikely to fully understand why gender inequalities persist over time.

HUMAN INVESTMENTS

Population dynamics are important for macroeconomics, but the issue of how to produce quality human beings goes well beyond simply counting the number of bodies. Equally important are the investments made in human development, things like education, emotional development and healthcare. Human investments jointly produce the physical organisms we call people and the capacities those people have to do things with their lives.

The previous section of this book argued that certain expenditures of time, money, and economic resources should be considered investments, although current macroeconomic measurements typically treat them as a type of consumption. These include investments in human development, such as health and educational services. They also include non-market, unpaid care services, often provided within the household. Why should these services be classified as investment? Physical investments in capital goods, such as machines, computers, equipment, roads, power infrastructure, etc., increase the productivity and productive capacity of the economy. An investment made now yields returns, in terms of greater productivity, in the future. Similarly, investments in human beings help sustain and improve their future productivity. The major difference is that these human investments are less tangible, and often involve services rather than goods.

Economics has a long history of focusing primarily on material production. Much economic theory sees the driving force of economic growth under a capitalist system to be the accumulation of physical, productive goods that are grouped under the catch-all heading of "capital". Because services are intangible, they have received less attention. Services only last for a specific period of time and they cannot be stored the same way that physical products can. Because of this, economic theory often assumes that services cannot be investments. Investment is primarily seen as involving the production of long-lasting goods that raise the productivity of economic activities in the future.

This is a mistake. Although services themselves are intangible and fleeting, the effects of consuming services can be long lasting and affect future productivity. Imagine that you enrolled in a short course that lasted three hours a week for four weeks in order to learn how to use a piece of software important for your job. The service that is being offered, software instruction, only lasts for a set period of time, in this case 12 hours spread over four weeks. However, the skills that are developed by consuming this service last much longer. They also would make you more productive at your job. They represent a type of investment.

As has already been discussed, investments of time, money, and economic resources are essential for reproduction of the workforce and the long-run sustainability of an economy. Demographic shifts also have implications for the trajectory of economic development, in ways we do not always fully understand. But these kinds of human investments also affect other factors that contribute to overall economic performance. In many models, technology is a central determinant of productivity and living standards. However, the production of technology, the creation of new knowledge and ideas, requires investments in the human beings that come up with those new ideas and generate knowledge.[6] It is hard to imagine economies, particularly modern economies, functioning without these human investments.

There is one category of intangible investments that economists have long recognized: education. Investments in skills, knowledge and know-how, grouped under the heading "human capital", are seen as similar to investments in physical capital (Becker 1994). The accumulation of knowledge and skills enhances people's productive contribution. At the individual level, greater productivity justifies paying more highly educated people more money. At the macroeconomic level, investments that raise formal educational attainment or build new skills support economic growth.

The idea that education represents a type of investment has generated a great deal of literature that attempts to understand the returns to that investment. Investment in physical capital raises future productivity and, as a result, generates returns on that investment in the form of more production and additional earnings. Along the same lines, investments in education should generate similar returns if such investments enhance future productivity. The evidence shows that this is the case. A review of over 1,100 studies across a range of countries (139 in total) found that the global average of the returns to an extra year of schooling were approximately 9 per cent. In other words, having one more year of schooling would raise future earnings by 9 per cent (Psacharopoulos & Patrinos 2018). As long as the cost of that extra year of education is less than the total present value of the increase in earnings, investing in more education makes economic sense, that is, if we only value education in terms of its effects on a person's earning power.

---

6. In Paul Romer's classic model of economic growth with endogenous technological change, human capital is the only input into the production of new knowledge; see Romer 1990.

For instance, if a person in the US were earning $50,000 a year and returns to education were 9 per cent, an additional year of schooling would raise those earnings to $54,500 – an additional $4,500 a year for the rest of that person's working life. The total monetary value of that extra year of education to that individual would be $4,500 per year accumulated over time, with future amounts adjusted for the prevailing interest rate to take into account the fact that if money were not spent on an additional year of education, it could have earned a return equal to the interest rate. If the person worked 20 years after getting the extra year of schooling and interest rates were zero, the monetary value of that additional education would be $4,500 x 20 years = $90,000. In contrast, if the prevailing interest rate were 5 per cent, the total money value would be discounted to approximately $56,000 to account for the fact that $4,500 today is worth more than $4,500 20 years from now, since money received today could have been invested at 5 per cent interest.[7]

Most estimates of the returns to education only look at private returns. Private returns represent the money value of higher individual earnings associated with additional education. But education also generates social returns. We all benefit, to some degree, by being part of a more educated community. Working alongside someone with special skills could have knock-on effects, as other, less-skilled employees pick up knowledge from their colleagues. Innovations arising out of more educational investments can benefit everyone. Social returns are not adequately captured by the standard measures of returns to education. Currently, our understanding of these social returns is limited. There have been some efforts to measure at least some aspects of the social returns to education and this research tends to show that social returns exceed private returns (e.g. Acemoglu & Angrist 1999).

The idea that education represents a kind of intangible capital investment that raises productivity and generates future returns has found its way into macroeconomic growth theories (e.g. Barro 2001; Mankiw, Romer & Weil 1992). These theories typically only include measurements

---

7. This is simply the present value of a stream of payments equal to $4,500 made at the end of the year for 20 years at 5 per cent interest.

of formal educational attainment as an indicator of human capital. Other types of human investments are usually not considered. For instance, certain types of health services have the potential to raise productivity in the long run, by allowing people to live longer, healthier and therefore more productive lives. Yet even if formal health services were integrated into macroeconomic models, it would represent an incomplete accounting of human investments.

This is because investments in human capital are often narrowly defined to include activities that take place within the market economy or in the public sector. In other words, only those activities that would be included in the traditional definition and measurement of GDP are considered to contribute to human capital formation. But many contributions that are made to health and education take place outside of the market economy and involve unpaid care work, as the previous section of this book argued. What we miss when we focus only on formal health and educational services measured in the system of national accounts are all of the human investments associated with non-market production.

To demonstrate this point, it helps to give an example. One important area of human investment in which non-market production plays a substantial role is early childhood development. Numerous research studies show that investments in early childhood development affect cognitive development, educational achievement later in life and health outcomes. All of these outcomes have important consequences for overall economic performance (Heckman 1999, 2013; Alderman 2011; Naudeau, Martinez & Filmer 2011). Unpaid care work is central to investment in early childhood development, although its contribution and the importance of gender roles are not always recognized. Direct interactions between children and caregivers – including speech, gestures, facial expressions, physical contact and body movements – provide the stimulation necessary for children's cognitive development (Bornstein *et al.* 2008). This kind of direct care represents a critical component of non-market human investments that have implications for the long-run health of an economy.

Because of the unequal burden of unpaid care work, this raises a challenge for designing policies that support positive outcomes for children as well as for gender equality. Care work is necessary to the investment in human beings required to support a viable macroeconomic environment. However, the current distribution of this work between women and men is highly unequal and it entrenches women's unequal position in the economy. In order to incorporate unpaid care work into the formulation of macroeconomic policies in ways that actually reduce gender inequalities, policies need to be designed in such a way as to reduce and redistribute unpaid work. We will return to this issue.

MACROECONOMICS ACROSS GENERATIONS

Macroeconomic theory, particularly mainstream approaches to understanding consumption and savings, have recognized that people make different choices at distinct junctures in their lives. Much of this theory focuses on how adult individuals make spending decisions throughout the lifecycle. Economists have long noted that young adults frequently spend more than they receive in income. They borrow against future earnings, taking out loans for college, a car, or buying their first house. As they grow older and their incomes rise, they tend to pay off these loans, borrow less, and save more. Income exceeds consumption and wealth grows as individuals accumulate savings. At some point, people typically reach an age when they stop working. They draw on the money they saved to finance consumption in old age.

Back in the 1950s, the economist Franco Modigliani, together with his student Richard Brumberg, first proposed the life-cycle hypothesis of consumption (Modigliani & Brumberg 1954). Their basic idea was that people try to smooth consumption over their lifetimes, even when the amount they earn varies with their age. They consume more than they earn when they are young and when they retire, and consume less than they earn during their prime working years. The sum of these individual decisions across all people of various ages would determine total household consumption and savings at the macro level at a particular moment in time. Within this theoretical world, individuals are forward-looking and expert planners. The amount they spend in one year is based, not on that year's income, but on their expected earnings throughout their entire lives.

One drawback of this theory is that it downplays economic interactions between people of different generations. Consumption and savings decisions are entirely based on the choices of autonomous adults motivated by their own self-interest. Different generations certainly co-exist. There will be young people, prime working-age adults, and retired individuals, all with different patterns of savings and consumption. Adding up all these individual decisions yields aggregate consumption and savings. But, importantly, under the life-cycle hypothesis, people make their spending and savings choices as isolated individuals. The decisions of one generation do not affect the choices available to other generations, and people only consider the enjoyment of their own consumption when making spending choices. This is a convenient simplification with important limitations. For instance, children do not fit well into this picture. To deal with kids within the confines of the lifecycle hypothesis, it helps to assume that children represent a type of consumer good and the decision to have kids is simply one consumer choice out of many.

Ignoring the interactions between generations generates some potential problems for classic macroeconomic thinking. The influential economist, Paul Samuelson, pointed out some of these tensions around the same time that the life-cycle hypothesis was first being developed (Samuelson 1958). Consider the following thought experiment. Imagine an economy with a population divided into two generations: (1) the working-age generation and (2) an older retired, or non-working, generation. The working-age generation produces the goods and services that make up GDP. The non-working generation produces nothing. This is a simple barter economy, in which all exchanges involve produced goods and services. Moreover, the goods and services produced have a shelf-life of just one generation. For instance, food purchased when people are in their 30s will not last until the time they retire.

Samuelson asked the following question: in such an economy, how would the retired generation be able to stake a claim to the goods and services produced by the working-age generation? They still need food, clothing, housing, and other necessities, but do not produce these things themselves. Since the retired generation has no income and they cannot carry-over consumption from the time when they were working, providing for the older population requires that the current generation give up a portion of what they produce. But why would the current working-age population forego consumption of what they produce in order to free up some goods and services for the older generation?

Samuelson argued that relying on individual self-interest is not enough to solve this problem. Social institutions or some form of social contract is needed. One social institution that helps solve this problem is money. Money is a particular type of commodity that, if it is stable, holds its value across generations. The working-age generation may forego some consumption when they are employed and save some of their income in the form of money (or in the form of a financial asset that has a monetary value). When they eventually retire and no longer have income, they can use the money they have saved to stake a claim to the goods and services they need out of current production. This is not too different from the life-cycle hypothesis, as long as money, a specific type of social institution, exists.

But relying on private savings and financial assets is not the only way to address this problem. Another possible solution to the dilemma described by Samuelson is to develop some kind of agreement, a social contract, between the two generations. The current working-age generation would give up some of the goods and services they produce and make these available to the older generation. They are only willing to do this because there would be an agreement, explicit or implicit, that would guarantee that the working-age population would enjoy the same treatment when they eventually retire. This arrangement is similar to a "pay-as-you-go" pension system, like the US Social Security Program. Under a pay-as-you-go pension, the current working-age generation is taxed in order to provide income support to the retired generation. This effectively reduces the consumption of the working-age generation in order to free up goods and services to support people in their retirement.

All of this is fairly sensible and much of macroeconomic theory focuses on how adults make consumption and savings decisions within a particular institutional context. One group of macroeconomic theories, called overlapping generations (OLG) models, specifically explores how these choices are made when populations are comprised of distinct generations.[8] In this regard, the OLG approaches represent an alternative to the life-cycle hypothesis and its variants. Macroeconomic theory could simply rest there, with these alternative theories of long-run consumption and savings. But there is an important omission. Most of these theories of adult decision-making fail to consider what it takes for a person to become an adult in the first place. There is a missing generation.

CHILDREN AND MACROECONOMICS

The simple two-generation macroeconomic model gets more complicated when we introduce a third generation: children. Children represent another non-working population. Like the older, non-working population, they require a share of the currently produced goods and services to survive and grow into adulthood. As this book has repeatedly stressed, part of the services they require are produced outside of the market economy, uncounted in macroeconomic statistics and based on the unpaid care work performed primarily by women. How do we insure that children get the goods and services they need? The question is similar to the one posed by Samuelson with regard to the retired generation. However, now the social institution of money is of little help. Children have no prior savings and typically command no financial assets.

Once again, relying on pure self-interest fails to solve the problem. Adults who raise children must forgo a certain amount of consumption, since some fraction of household income goes to purchase goods and services the children need. Furthermore, the unpaid labour dedicated to caring for kids could have generated income in the labour market. In this respect, it also represents a form of foregone consumption. Purely self-interested people would not do something that was costly to

---

8. A classic example of an OLG model can be found in Peter Diamond, "National Debt in a Neoclassical Growth Model", *American Economic Review* 55(5) (1965): 1126–50.

themselves (i.e. lower their consumption) in order to help someone else (i.e. children). Different motivations and social institutions come into play.

One explanation for why people have children that is consistent with purely self-interested motivations is that people see children as a type of old-age insurance. A purely self-interested parent may spend time and money raising children if they are guaranteed that their children will return the favour and support them when they are older and unable to work. According to this argument, children only have instrumental value. They are the means through which parents maintain a certain lifestyle and level of consumption in old age. This arrangement requires an implicit social contract in which children are obligated to repay their parents for the economic resources that allowed them to grow into productive adults. There is a certain amount of truth do this argument. Children often feel a commitment to help their aging parents. But it is doubtful that this intergenerational contract is sufficient to insure that pure self-interest will guarantee that society will reproduce itself over time.

One problem with this story is that it assumes that the social contract is enforceable, and enforceable at zero or low cost to the parents. If we assume that parents are motivated by pure self-interest, there is no reason to believe that their children will behave differently. But self-interested children have a strong motivation to renege on the social contract when the time comes to cough up serious time and money for their parents. This problem has long been recognized. Shakespeare even made it the subject of one of his tragedies. In *King Lear*, Lear decides to divide up his kingdom among his three daughters based on how much they say they love him. His two oldest daughters profess their love and get generous shares. Lear's youngest daughter refuses to indulge him and is disinherited. It does not take long for the two older daughters and their husbands to turn against King Lear, and he ends up destitute, eventually going insane.

Self-interest creeps into decisions about whether to have children or not (e.g. "who will take care of me when I'm old?"), but it is unlikely to be a sufficient motivation. Most parents, if asked, would say they love their kids and that they would make sacrifices to help their children enjoy a decent life. These parents are not motivated by pure self-interest, but rather some degree of altruism. Some biologists argue that human beings, like other living things, are driven to reproduce in order to insure their genes are replicated and survive in the next generation (Dawkins 1990). They are willing to make personal sacrifices in order to insure their offspring have the best chance possible.

But there is more to it than biology. People have different preferences when it comes to having a family. Some really want children, others do not. Social norms also come into play. In some societies, there is enormous pressure on women to marry and have children. They may have few economic opportunities outside of a traditional patriarchal marriage, so raising a family becomes their primary economic role. Social norms also help enforce social contracts. Parents that neglect their children may face disapproval from the community in which they live. Similarly, children may be expected, under prevailing social conventions, to take their aging parents into their homes.

So why do people have children? There is no simple answer. The explanation involves a combination of different motivations, preferences, biology, social norms, and institutions (Folbre 1994a). Economics also comes into play. The cost of raising children varies over time and across countries. Kids are not cheap – as was made clear in the estimates of the value of unpaid childcare discussed earlier in the book. When women have children, economic factors influence their choices, imperfectly and with many uncertainties.

This creates serious coordination challenges when it comes to macroeconomics. As discussed earlier, some countries, with large youthful populations, may benefit from falling fertility rates and greater investment in each individual child. Other economies are facing the potentially daunting prospect of below-replacement fertility and aging populations. Demographic change has consequences for the macroeconomy, yet there is no automatic mechanism for coordinating the demographic needs of the economy at the macro-level with the choices regarding childbearing and investments in children at the level of the family or with regard to individual women. To put it another way, there is no guarantee that fertility rates will somehow miraculously respond in a way that will produce the best economic outcomes in the absence of purposeful economic policies or the right social institutions.

Recall that Thomas Malthus had proposed a mechanism whereby population growth rates would respond to changing macroeconomic conditions. He argued that, as incomes grew, fertility rates would also increase. As the number of people rose relative to the productive resources available, average incomes would stop rising and begin to fall. According to Malthus, this downward pressure on incomes would eventually lead to starvation and higher mortality rates. In other words, macroeconomic outcomes would respond in such a way as to stabilize population growth rates. The Malthus correction is a clever idea, but looking back at the history of economic development, there is little reason to put much stock in his original argument.

There is another class of coordination challenges associated with social reproduction. Not everyone has children or contributes equally to raising the next generation. Yet there are broad-based benefits to insuring that the economy has the human resources it needs to keep functioning. At the macro-level, the long-run health of the economy depends on it. This suggests that while most people will benefit from investments made in children, only some bear the costs of raising the next generation (Folbre 1994b). This creates what economists call a "free-rider" problem – not everyone who benefits from these social investments pays their fair share.

The possibility of a free-rider problem is best illustrated with an example. Consider a pay-as-you-go pension scheme in which the current working-age population is taxed in order to finance a pension for the retired population. For the sake of simplicity, assume that the entire retired population gets income support. In this example, all retirees get an income grant that depends on the productive activities of the working-age population. But not all retired people had children, and not all of them spent the time and money needed to raise the current working-age population to adulthood. This generates built-in inequalities. Parents with children would have forgone a certain amount of income and consumption in order to invest in their kids. But people with no kids also benefit from these investments without bearing the same costs. There is a gender dimension to these distributive dynamics when mothers disproportionately bear the costs of raising the next generation. These gender inequalities are intensified if, thanks to the design of the pension scheme, women receive a lower payment because they spent less time in paid employment and more time providing unpaid care services.

As this book has argued, the costs of raising the next generation are sizable. These costs are not fixed, they change over time, and expectations of these costs influence women's decisions whether to have children or not. There are numerous components to the cost of children. Part of the costs involve direct spending – the money that goes towards the children's food, clothing, education, and healthcare, among other expenditures. Unpaid care work represents another component of the overall costs. Unpaid labour does not require a money exchange, but it still represents a real cost in terms of economic resources. The time spent caring for children could have been put to other uses, including earning more income in paid employment.

The cost of children tends to rise with long-run economic growth and development. For example, as average living standards increase, the average level of educational attainment also tends to rise. Back in the 1950s, in a country like the US, a high school education was sufficient to get a decent job. Now many parents expect that their children will attend a college or university. The statistics speak for themselves. In 1950, 33 per cent of the US population aged 25 years or more had completed at least four years of high school (14–18), but only 6 per cent had completed at least four years of higher education (college/university). In contrast, in 2017, 90 per cent had completed four years of high school and 34 per cent had completed four years of college.[9] This additional education can be expensive. Greater investment in educational outcomes increases the cost of raising a child to adulthood. Similarly, as wages and salaries increase, the opportunity costs of spending time in unpaid work, instead of paid employment, also grow. This further pushes up the cost of children.

---

9. The statistics come from the US Department of the Census.

Gender inequalities have an enormous impact on the cost of children – and who ends up paying those costs? When women perform the majority of unpaid care work, the opportunity cost of their labour, what they could have earned in paid employment, becomes an important contributor to the overall cost of children. Large inequalities in the labour market, with women earning just a fraction of what men earn, effectively lowers the costs of children when women are the ones doing most of the unpaid care work. These kinds of pay gaps reinforce the gender division of labour and entrench gender inequalities. If the goal is to keep the cost of raising children low, it makes sense for women to specialize in unpaid care work when there is a large gender pay gap. They give up less income than a man would by focusing on unpaid rather than paid work.

This implies that improvements in women's opportunities for paid employment will tend to push up the cost of children. This is not necessarily just a one-time cost involving more unpaid labour when the kids are young. Women who take time off to have children may end up interrupting their career tracks, and this can affect their long-run earnings throughout the rest of their working lives (see, e.g., Blau & Kahn 2016; Kleven, Landais & Søgaard 2018).

Women are the ones that have children, but their decision to do so occurs within a complex social and economic environment. Putting aside social norms that prescribe women's role as one of childbearing, raising a child on one's own is an expensive proposition. It is not surprising that women often have children within some kind of partnership, such as a marriage or cohabitating arrangement. Pooling labour allows one partner, often a man, to specialize in paid employment while the other spends more time doing unpaid work. Forming a household also saves money. Two adults can live together in a single house or apartment. They do not need separate residences. They can cook together and share household durables, such as a car, a stove or a washing machine. Because of this, average costs per person of maintaining a family are lower the more people, adults and children, live under one roof – as long as they share, at least to some extent, their resources (Folbre 2008). These economies of scale make it less costly to raise children in some form of partnership than it would for a mother to do it alone.

However, there are potential downsides to women having children within a partnership. Men may be in a stronger position than women when it comes to making decisions about how economic resources are used. In other words, men have a stronger bargaining position. Consider two-person "breadwinner" households, in which men do paid work and earn all the income and women specialize in unpaid household work. Since men earn the household's income, they may have more influence on how it is used. Women who do only unpaid work have limited exit options. If they leave their partners, how will they earn the income needed for themselves and their children? When women lack a strong fallback position, it weakens their bargaining power.

How does bargaining power influence the distribution of the costs of children? Raising children in a two-adult (or more) household lowers the costs of children, for the reasons already discussed. But those costs may be unequally shared, with women bearing more of those costs than men. This increases the costs to women of having children, although perhaps not enough to make women want to go it alone and raise their children themselves. When there is unequal bargaining power, men's share of the costs of having children will likely be reduced. They enjoy the benefits of knowing that there will be a next generation without paying the same price as women.

There is another risk with forming a household and having children within a partnership. Marriages and other cohabiting relationships do not necessarily last forever. When they collapse, it is common for women to take primary responsibility for the children. The benefits of sharing these costs, and the economies of scale associated with having a multiple-adult household, evaporate. Because of this, the costs of children increase and a large part of the burden of higher costs falls on the mothers. A system that enforces child support payments would help to offset the rise in costs, but such payments are not always forthcoming and enforcement may be weak. Because of this, the costs of children to women will likely rise when there is a fall in the likelihood that marriages and other partnerships will last.

All of this means that single-mothers are likely to be, on average, more vulnerable than women who raise children in other arrangements. This pushes up the cost of children to these women and the expected costs to other mothers, since there is a chance that mothers in partnerships will end up having to go it alone if those partnerships dissolve. But there are several paths to single motherhood. Women may choose to have and raise children alone. They would face higher costs and would have fewer opportunities to share those costs than mothers in partnerships. But they would have greater autonomy and control over decisions within the household.

All of this is to say that the structure of households matters for determining the costs of children and who bears those costs. Changes in the composition of households or in the likelihood that partnerships persist affect the costs of children. Shifts in bargaining power, for instance if women's economic opportunities outside the home improve, affect the distribution of those costs. These dynamics, in turn, affect fertility rates, investments in children, and demographics – all of which have macroeconomic implications. However, few macroeconomic frameworks even consider these issues.

Traditional patriarchal institutions structure the costs of children, the distribution of those costs, and fertility choices in a specific way. Consider a situation in which most women have few economic opportunities outside of the home; in which stigma against divorce and extramarital childbearing is strong; and in which bargaining power within the household strongly favours men. Under these conditions, women will feel pressure to marry and have children. Unequal bargaining power shifts the burden of those costs onto women, to the benefit of men. Since women have few alternative economic opportunities, the relative cost of children is kept low. Lower costs of children help support a higher fertility rate, and help insure the reproduction of the next generation, including the future workforce. Adding it all up yields demographic changes at the macroeconomic level that affect the future trajectory of the economy.

Traditional patriarchal institutions characterize some societies. In others, the institutions and norms are different or have changed over time. Marriage rates may fall, and divorce rates rise. The number of single-mother households may grow over time. Women's opportunities for good jobs and educational opportunities give them options apart from taking up typical gender roles. Norms and attitudes can shift, so that men take greater responsibility for raising children. Countries may introduce family support policies, such as maternity leave and public childcare options, that provide support outside of historic patriarchal structures. As argued earlier, these changes have implications for demographics and long-run economic performance.

It is also important to remember that not all households are the same. The quality of investments made in children will be correlated with households' socio-economic status, providing a channel for the transmission of poverty and inequality across generations (Engle *et al.* 2011; Irwin, Siddiqi & Hertzman 2007). In order to prevent social inequalities deepening over time, macroeconomic policies need to support adequate investment in the childhood development of low-income households. Societies that are polarized by extreme, or growing, income inequality may make insufficient investments in future generations, particularly when household resources are squeezed in families with children. Under these circumstances, there is a justification to take steps to support adequate human investments, especially among lower-income households.

AN EQUITABLE MACROECONOMICS FOR THE LONG HAUL

The reproduction of society from one generation to the next represents a critical aspect of a sustainable economy. Social reproduction goes beyond simply insuring that there are enough human bodies to constitute a future labour force. It requires substantial investment in human capacities. These investments involve market and non-market services. Such services tend to be seen as intangible and ephemeral, but they have long-lasting effects on the well-being of individuals and their families. They produce real value that defies measurement solely in the metric of money and market exchange. They determine what people are able to become and what contributions they are able to make in the course of their lives. In a real sense, they underpin the health of the macroeconomy.

Yet the institutions and arrangements that support the reproduction of society and the long-run sustainability of the economy are not always just or fair. This is reflected, for example, in women's unequal burden of unpaid work, a major source of structural inequality. And so we come full circle to where this book began. Economic policies and institutions have gender specific effects because they interact with and, at times, reinforce existing structural sources of inequality. A more equitable macroeconomics would need to not only acknowledge, but assist in transforming, these underlying inequalities.

4

Revamping macroeconomics so that people count

Macroeconomics needs to take people more seriously. Human beings represent the most important economic resource that undergirds long-run economic performance and well-being. It is not just the sheer number of people on the planet that counts. Their capacities to contribute to their households, communities, and their societies are of utmost importance. Moreover, human beings are products of the economies in which they live. Raising children to adulthood requires substantive investments of time, money, goods and services. It also requires coordinating the allocation of resources across generations.

This coordination does not happen by magic, or exclusively through markets or pure self-interest. Numerous institutions, including household structures, social norms, and gender roles, come into play. These institutions may not be fair. They may not be efficient. They often perpetuate inequalities, including economic disparities between men and women, and artificially limit women's potential by constraining their choices and options. Equally important, these institutions may not seamlessly adapt to the future needs of the economy. There is no guarantee that current demographic trends or investments in human beings will be sufficient to keep our economies healthy in the future.

Despite the importance of all of these issues, current macroeconomic thinking and practice falls short. This is dangerous, since the way we understand how the economy works influences the policies that are ultimately adopted. If our understanding is partial or impoverished, so will be our solutions to the problems we face.

What is also clear is that the exact mix of policies and institutions needed will vary from one context to the next. Some countries fear the consequences of below-replacement fertility, as their populations age and slowly shrink. Others, with high fertility rates, face the challenge of what to do with a burgeoning youth population. Social norms and gender roles differ, as do the structures of economies. No single solution exists for all people and places. There is no "one size fits all" option. Nevertheless, we can discuss what the elements of a better macroeconomics might look like.

So, what are the key ingredients of a revitalized macroeconomics? Reworking basic concepts and measurements is a good place to start. This book explained in detail how including non-market production and redefining key variables, such as savings and investment, alters macroeconomic analysis. In many circumstances, we may not yet have precise measurements of the value of non-market production and human investments generated through unpaid work. But this does not prohibit us from considering these factors in macroeconomic models and moving closer to better measurements and indicators.

The production of human beings and their capabilities is an issue of critical macroeconomic importance. With the exception of the idea of human capital, defined narrowly as consisting of formal education and skills, these kinds of investments have not found their way into most macroeconomic models. It is still commonplace to treat human beings as non-produced factors of production and demographic trends as external to the macroeconomy.

Taking the idea of human investment seriously broadens the scope of macroeconomic policy. Typically, policies that impact on education, health, or households' living standards are labelled social policies and are subordinate to macroeconomics. Only after the macroeconomic parameters have been set do policy-makers decide which social policies are feasible. This is backwards. By acknowledging that human investments have macroeconomic consequences, an array of social policies are elevated to the status of macroeconomic policies, including aspects of education, health and childcare policies. Unpaid work, disproportionately done by women, becomes a critical factor of production, one that has been necessary to sustain our economies in the long run.

This book began with a consideration of the distributive consequences of macroeconomic policies, the idea that macro policies have different effects on women and men because of structural sources of gender inequality. If macroeconomic policies are to contribute to greater gender equality, these unequal outcomes need to be taken into account. Moreover, macroeconomic policies are instrumental in mobilizing the resources, through taxation and other sources of public revenues, necessary to support policies and programmes that aim to reduce structural inequalities between women and men (UN Women 2015).

Generating additional tax revenue to finance specific government programmes has not always been welcomed. Taxes represent a transfer of resources from private households and businesses to governments. If increases in government expenditures are entirely offset by less private spending, the net effect is potentially unclear and may be zero. This is the familiar crowding-out argument. But crowding-out assumes that government spending has no effect on the productivity of market and non-market activities. In other words, it assumes the size of the economic pie to be fixed. But, as discussed at length, certain types of government expenditures, particular those that invest in human capacities, enhance private productivity and, instead of consuming scarce resources, mitigate scarcity by generating new resources. They actually grow the economic pie. Under these conditions, the crowding-out argument begins to crumble. We can imagine gender equitable approaches to government spending, from public childcare to opening up educational opportunities, that have these kinds of positive long-run consequences.

The idea that investing in gender equality may be good for the economy is not new, but these arguments often focus narrowly on policies that may boost women's productive contribution, often defined only in terms of the market economy. But there is another, insidious connection between gender inequality and macroeconomics that needs to be addressed. Gender inequalities underpin the traditional institutions that insure the reproduction of the next generation and the continuity of the world's economies. By quite literally taking these factors out of the equation, macroeconomics contributes to perpetuating the current situation. Measuring women's contribution in terms of unpaid work is important, but it is simply not enough. Accounting for this labour does not change the fact that the unequal burden of non-market work is a major contributor to gender inequality.

This raises some major contradictions. Efforts to reduce gender inequality combined with weakening or shifting patriarchal institutions should improve women's economic position and their bargaining power. These changes would also disrupt the traditional ways in which social reproduction and investments in the next generation have been coordinated. Women may delay having children or forego childbearing altogether. Marriage rates may fall with more children being raised outside of stable partnerships. As the number of non-traditional households increases, the costs of raising the next generation would become more unequally distributed across different household types. These inequalities would contribute to unequal investments in children, since the resources available to families with kids differ. All of these developments have potentially serious implications for the future trajectory of the economy.

Gender inequalities have supported economic growth and development for a long time. Because of this, messing with the underlying institutions of social reproduction will have macroeconomic consequences. This is not to suggest that gender inequality is simply an unfortunate fact of life. Rather it is to point out that as traditional institutions begin to change, they need to be replaced by new ways of coordinating the reproduction of the next generation in ways that are gender equitable. This could include maternity and paternity leave policies, the extension of the public school system to include preschool, the development of public and subsidized childcare programmes, programmes to encourage the equal sharing of care work between men and women, the introduction of policies to equalize investments in children regardless of household income or structure, and family support grants – unconditional payments to caregivers that acknowledge the large costs involved in raising children.

The development of a more gender equitable system for investing in the next generation is more likely to happen if we had macroeconomic theories, models, and policies that took these issues seriously. A reworked macroeconomics must recognize that goods and services are not the only things produced within an economic system. People, and their capacity to do things with their lives, are perhaps the most valuable creation of our economic system. We need to transform macroeconomics so that it recognizes this reality.

References

Acemoglu, D. & J. Angrist 1999. "How large are the social returns to education? Evidence from compulsory schooling laws", NBER working paper 7444. Cambridge, MA: National Bureau of Economic Research.

Agénor, P.-R. 2017. "A computable overlapping generations model for gender and growth policy analysis". *Macroeconomic Dynamics* 21, 11–54.

Alderman, H. (ed.) 2011. *No Small Matter: The Impact of Poverty, Shocks, and Human Capital Investment in Early Childhood Development*. Washington, DC: World Bank.

An, C.-B. & S.-H. Jeon 2006. "Demographic changes and economic growth in Korea". Paper presented at the 2006 Asia-Pacific Economics Association conference, Sungkyunkwan University and National Assembly Budget Office, Republic of Korea.

Barro, R. 2001. "Human capital and growth". *American Economic Review* 91(2), 12–17.

Barro, R. & G. Becker 1989. "Fertility choice in a model of economic growth". *Econometrica* 57(2), 481–501.

Becker, G. 1994. *Human Capital: A Theoretical and Empirical Analysis*. Third edition. Chicago, IL: University of Chicago Press.

Beneria, L. 1995. "Toward a greater integration of gender in economics". *World Development*, 23(11), 1839–50.

Berik, G. & E. Kongar 2015. "Time allocation of married mothers and fathers in hard times: the 2007–2009 US Recession". In S. Fukuda-Parr, J. Heintz & S. Seguino (eds), *Critical and Feminist Perspectives on Financial and Economic Crises*, {pages}. London: Routledge.

Bibler, S. & E. Zuckerman 2013. "The care connection: The World Bank and women's unpaid care work in select sub-Saharan African countries". WIDER working paper 2013/131. Helsinki: United Nations University.

Blau, F. & L. Kahn 2016. "The gender wage gap: extent, trends, and explanations". NBER working paper 21913. Cambridge, MA: National Bureau of Economic Research.

Bloom, D. & J. Finlay 2009. "Demographic change and economic growth in Asia". *Asian Economic Policy Review* 4(1), 45–64.

Bloom, D., D. Canning & J. Sevilla 2002. *The Demographic Dividend: A New Perspective on the Economic Consequences of Population Change*. Santa Monica, CA: RAND Corporation.

Blundell-Wignall, A. & P. Slovik 2011. "A market perspective on the European sovereign debt and banking crisis". *Financial Market Trends*, February, 1–28.

Bornstein, M., C. Tamis-Lemonda, C. Hahn & O. Haynes 2008. "Maternal responsiveness to young children at three ages: longitudinal analysis of a multidimensional, modular, and specific parenting construct". *Developmental Psychology* 44(3), 867–74.

Bos, F. 1992. *The History of National Accounting*. National Accounts Research Division, Central Bureau of Statistics, The Netherlands.

Bowles, S. & H. Gintis 1993. "The revenge of Homo economicus: contested exchange and the revival of political economy". *Journal of Economic Perspectives* 7(1), 83–102.

Braunstein, E., I. van Staveren & D. Tavani 2011. "Embedding care and unpaid work in macroeconomic modeling: a structuralist approach". *Feminist Economics* 17(4), 5–31.

Braunstein, E. & J. Heintz 2008. "Gender bias and central bank policy: employment and inflation reduction". *International Review of Applied Economics* 22(2), 173–86.

BEA (Bureau of Economic Analysis) 2017. *Concepts and Methods of the US National Income and Product Accounts*. Washington DC: US Department of Commerce.

Chang, H.-J. & I. Grabel 2014. *Reclaiming Development: An Alternative Economic Policy Manual*. London: Zed Books.

CMEPSP (Commission on the Measurement of Economic Performance and Social Progress) 2010. *Mismeasuring Our Lives: Why GDP Doesn't Add Up*, J. Stiglitz, A. Sen & J.-P. Fitoussi (eds). New York: The New Press.

Cordero, J. & J. Montecino 2010. "Capital controls and monetary policy in developing countries". Research report. Washington, DC: Center for Economic and Policy Research.

Dawkins, R. 1990. *The Selfish Gene*. Oxford: Oxford University Press.

Doepke, M. & M. Tertilt 2016. "Families in macroeconomics". NBER working paper No. 22068. Cambridge, MA: National Bureau of Economic Research.

Dollar, D. & R. Gatti 1999. *Gender Inequality, Income and Growth: Are Good Times Good for Women?* Washington DC: World Bank.

Duflo, E. 2012. "Women empowerment and economic development". *Journal of Economic Literature* 50(4), 1051–79.

Elson, D. 1998. "Integrating gender issues into national budgetary policies and procedures: some policy options". *Journal of International Development* 10, 929–41.

Elson, D. 1995. "Gender awareness in modeling structural adjustment". *World Development* 23(11), 1851–68.

Epstein, G. & E. Yeldan 2008. "Inflation targeting, employment creation, and economic development: assessing the impacts and policy alternatives". *International Review of Applied Economics* 22(2), 131–44.

Folbre, N. 2008. *Valuing Children: Rethinking the Economics of the Family.* Cambridge, MA: Havard University Press.

Folbre, N. 1994a. *Who Pays for the Kids? Gender and the Structure of Constraint.* London: Routledge.

Folbre, N. 1994b. "Children as public goods". *American Economic Review* 84(2), 86–90.

Galor, O. & D. Weil 1996. "The gender gap, fertility, and growth". *American Economic Review* 86(3), 374–87.

Grown, C. & I. Valodia 2010. *Taxation and Gender Equity: A Comparative Analysis of Direct and Indirect Taxes in Developing and Developed Countries.* London: Routledge.

Harrod, R. 1939. "An essay in dynamic theory". *The Economic Journal* 49(193), 14–33.

Heckman, J. 1999. "Policies to foster human capital". NBER working paper No. 7288. Cambridge, MA: National Bureau of Economic Research.

Heckman, J. 2013. "The economics of inequality and human development". Keynote presentation at the First National Congress meeting on Building a Legal Framework for Public Policies for Early Childhood, Brasilia, 16 April.

ILO (International Labour Organization) 2018. *Care Work and Care Jobs for the Future of Decent Work.* Geneva: ILO.

IMF (International Monetary Fund) 2013. *Key Aspects of Macroprudential Policies.* Washington, DC: IMF.

Jones, C. 1997. "Population and ideas: a theory of endogenous growth". NBER working paper No. 6285. Cambridge, MA: National Bureau of Economic Research.

Kabeer, N. & L. Natali 2013. "Gender equality and economic growth: is there a win-win?". IDS working paper 417. Falmer: Institute of Development Studies.

Kaldor, N. 1957. "A model of economic growth". *The Economic Journal* 67(268), 591–624.

Karamessini, M. 2014. "Structural crisis and adjustment in Greece: social regression and the challenge to gender equality". In M. Karamessini & J. Rubery (eds), *Women and Austerity. The Economic Crisis and the Future for Gender Equality*, 165–85. Routledge: London.

Klasen, S. & F. Lamanna 2009. "The impact of gender inequality in education and employment on economic growth: new evidence for a panel of countries". *Feminist Economics* 15(3), 91–132

Kleven, H., C. Landais & J. Søgaard 2018. "Children and gender inequality: evidence from Denmark". NBER working paper 24219. Cambridge, MA: National Bureau of Economic Research.

Lim, C. *et al.* 2011. *Macroprudential Policy: What Instruments and How to Use Them? Lessons from Country Experiences*. Washington, DC: IMF.

Malthus, T. [1798] 2004. *An Essay on the Principle of Population*. New York: Norton.

Mankiw, N., D. Romer & D. Weil 1992. "A contribution to the empirics of economic growth". *Quarterly Journal of Economics* 107(2), 407–37.

Maruthappu, M. *et al.* 2014. "The association between government healthcare spending and maternal mortality in the European Union, 1981–2010: a retrospective study". *BJOG: An International Journal of Obstetrics & Gynecology* 122, 1216–24.

Masiyiwa, G. 2017. "Zimbabwe's economic collapse cited in rise of gender-based violence". *Global Press Journal*, 21 July. Available at: https://global pressjournal.com/africa/zimbabwe/zimbabwes-economic-collapse-cited-rise-gender-based-violence/ (accessed 29 October 2018).

Modigliani, F. & R. Brumberg 1954. "Utility analysis and the consumption function: an interpretation of cross-section data". In K. Kurihara (ed.), *Post-Keynesian Economics*, 388–436. New Brunswick, NJ. Rutgers University Press.

Montaño, S. & V. Milosavljevic 2012. "The economic and financial crisis: its impact on poverty, work, and women's time". Serie Mujer y Desarrollo. ECLAC (CEPAL). Santiago: Division for Gender Affairs.

Naudeau, S. *et al.* 2011. "Cognitive development among young children in low-income countries". In H. Alderman (ed.), *No Small Matter: The Impact of Poverty, Shocks and Human Capital Investment in Early Childhood Development*. Washington, DC: World Bank.

Peng, I. 2012. "The boss, the worker, his wife, and no babies: South Korean political and social economy of care in a context of institutional rigidities".

In S. Razavi & S. Staab (eds), *Global Variations in the Political and Social Economy of Care: Worlds Apart* {pages}. London: Routledge

Psacharopoulos, G. & H. Patrinos 2018. "Returns to investment in education : a decennial review of the global literature". Policy Research working paper; no. WPS 8402. Washington, DC: World Bank Group. Available at: http://documents.worldbank.org/curated/en/442521523465644318/Returns-to-investment-in-education-a-decennial-review-of-the-global-literature

Romer, P. 1990. "Endogenous technological change". *Journal of Political Economy* 98(5), 71–102.

Rubery, J. 2014. "From 'women and recession' to 'women and austerity': a framework for analysis". In M. Karamessini & J. Rubery (eds), *Women and Austerity. The Economic Crisis and the Future for Gender Equality*, 17–36. Routledge: London.

Samuelson, P. 1958. "An exact consumption-loan model of interest with or without the social contrivance of money". *Journal of Political Economy* 66(6), 467–82.

Seguino, S. & J. Heintz 2012. "Monetary tightening and the dynamics of US race and gender stratification". *American Journal of Economics and Sociology* 71(3), 603–38.

Seguino, S. 2000. "Gender inequality and economic growth: a cross-country analysis". *World Development* 28(7), 1211–30.

Solow, R. 1956. "A contribution to the theory of economic growth". *Quarterly Journal of Economics* 70(1), 65–94.

Stotsky, J. 2016. "Gender budgeting: fiscal context and current outcomes". IMF working paper WP/16/149. Washington DC: IMF.

Suh, J. & N. Folbre 2014. "Valuing unpaid child care in the USA: prototype satellite account using the American Time Use Survey". *Review of Income and Wealth* 62(4), 668–84.

Tachtamanova, Y. & E. Sierminska 2009. "Gender, monetary policy, and employment: the case of nine OECD countries". *Feminist Economics* 15(3), 323–53.

Tzannatos, Z. 1999. "Women and labor market changes in the global economy: growth helps, inequalities hurt and public policy matters". *World Development* 27(3), 551–69.

UN Women 2015. *Progress of the World's Women: Transforming Economies, Realizing Rights*. New York: UN Women.

Whitson, R. 2007. "Beyond the crisis: economic globalization and informal work in urban Argentina". *Journal of Latin American Geography* 6(2), 121–36.

Zandstra, D. 2011 "The European sovereign debt crisis and its evolving resolution". *Capital Markets Law Journal* 6(3), 285–316.

Index